To Cordelia, Malachy and my family and friends,
thank you for helping me during my time in need
and for allowing me to fulfil my dreams.

Ian McKinley has collaborated on his book with Gerry Thornley, Rugby Correspondent of The Irish Times. Thornley ghosted Trevor Brennan: Heart and Soul, which won the William Hill and Irish Book Awards Sport Book of the Year. Other books include the bestselling Ronan O'Gara: Unguarded, Front Up Rise Up: The Official Story of Connacht Rugby, Peter Stringer: Pulling The Strings and Seán O'Brien: Fuel, also shortlisted for the Bord Gáis Energy Irish Sports Book of the Year.

IAN McKINLEY
SECOND SIGHT
RUGBY AND REDEMPTION

WITH GERRY THORNLEY

Reach Sport

Reach Sport

Written with Gerry Thornley.

First published in Ireland and Great Britain in 2022 by Reach Sport.

www.reachsport.com
@Reach_Sport

Reach Sport is a part of Reach PLC.

Paperback ISBN: 9781914197499
eBook ISBN: 9781914197505

With thanks to Gill Hess Ltd.

Editor: Chris Brereton.

Photographic and text acknowledgements:
INPHO, Sportsfile, the Ian McKinley collection.
Diary excerpts included with the kind permission of the Belfast Telegraph.

Every effort has been made to trace copyright.
Any oversight will be rectified in future editions.

Printed and bound by CPI Group (UK) Ltd,
Croydon, CR0 4YY.

C O N T E N T S

An Inspiration And A Trailblazer

IAN IS four years younger than me so when he came into the Leinster academy in 2008 I had graduated into the senior squad a year beforehand on a development contract. But we're not worlds apart in terms of age.

I had heard of him in his schooldays. You often hear about good kids coming through the underage ranks, especially when they're not in one of the more established rugby playing schools, and looking at an Irish Schools' team sheet the name sticks out if they come from a school which isn't known for producing rugby players.

So when I saw Ian was playing for the Leinster and Irish

Schools' sides and came out of St Columba's I thought he must be a bit special.

When he came into the Leinster set-up I was immediately struck by how humble he was as a person, which was very refreshing. I quickly realised that this guy was different. I spent plenty of time kicking with Ian, and the other kickers, and he was keen to learn, very polite and just a nice person. He was very popular within the group. As a player I was immediately impressed by Ian's skill levels. He had a very good left boot and good game knowledge.

But half-way through his second season in the Leinster academy Ian suffered that terrible injury to his eye.

When word filtered through to the rest of the squad there were different rumours about the nature of the injury, how bad it was and how it happened. A group of us went in to visit him in the Royal Victoria Eye and Ear Hospital. It was one of the saddest visits I've ever made to a player in my career, to see someone who didn't know whether he would keep his sight in one eye, and especially for a player so young. If a player breaks a leg or an arm, it's not going to affect his life after rugby.

However, I remember how positive and upbeat Ian was when we visited him, which shocked us all.

Sure enough, Ian regained the sight in his eye and came back to play with us again the following season, by which stage Joe Schmidt had taken over from Michael Cheika. Joe really liked him. Ian might have been unsure of that but Joe usually gave guys he really rated a harder time, because he saw something in them. He wasn't as hard on the guys that he didn't rate so highly. Joe saw something in Ian and picked him to start a couple of games and he was on the bench in a few more when he came back in the second half of that 2010-11 season.

It looked like Ian had recovered fully, that the surgeons had done an amazing job, and so had he. We all presumed he was in the clear. Ian was being promoted to the senior squad the following season and he seemed set to have a long career with Leinster. I always had the sense with Ian that playing for Leinster was a huge deal for him. So, to have that hope suddenly taken away from him when he lost the sight in his eye, and then being forced to retire, must have been even more heartbreaking.

Ian moved away to Italy and that seemed like the end of his story as a rugby player. But, three years later there were reports of Ian playing again in Italy with the help of protective goggles. Then, on a Friday night in September 2016, more than five years after he had been forced to retire, we were sitting in the stands at the RDS and, along with everyone else, we applauded when Ian was introduced off the bench by Benetton for the last quarter, the first player in the professional game to play with protective goggles.

I can only recall playing against him once, briefly, in a Six Nations game in Rome in 2019, when he came on as a replacement a few minutes before Jack Carty replaced me to make his Irish debut.

I remember meeting Ian after a Leinster-Benetton game at a time when he was coaching and having a good catch-up with him. That was before his big comeback. We've stayed in touch through texts, usually before or after one of his games or one of mine, just to say well done or well played. I would have texted him before and after his Italian debut in November 2017.

For me, Ian's comeback demonstrated one thing above all else; how much he loves the game. His motivation wasn't financial, it was his pure love of rugby and a desire to get back playing again. To reach the professional level again and then to play Test rugby with Italy was remarkable.

It's bloody hard enough to play international rugby with two eyes, never mind with one. I could do with three eyes the odd time, to be honest, with people coming at you left, right and centre.

All I could do that night in September 2016, and any time I subsequently saw Ian play, was look on with admiration, especially when he played for Italy. What Ian has achieved in the game is unbelievable. He also had to mount a campaign off the pitch to gain permission to play with the protective goggles, a battle which he won. To learn how to play with one eye with the help of the goggles, and be good enough to earn a professional contract, only then to be refused permission to do so by various unions and federations must have been very upsetting for Ian and his family.

So, on several levels, like women's boxing being accepted in the Olympics, what Ian achieved was truly groundbreaking. Ian paved the way for every other player who needs goggles to play rugby.

He won a battle with himself to play the game, but also a battle for all those who might, one day, dream of following him. From start to finish, you couldn't have made up Ian's story, and it's a credit to him and his family that he showed such resolve and battled back from so many setbacks to be capped by his adopted country.

Ian has been an inspiration and a trailblazer.

ONE

Why Me?

Saturday 16th January 2010.

MY TEAM, UCD, have a top of the table AIL Division 2 clash against Lansdowne at the UCD Bowl. Kick-off is 2.30.

I prepare for the game as I usually would.

I'm awake and up by 9am. That's a relative lie-in compared with weekdays in the Leinster Academy, when I am usually up at 6am.

I have my normal matchday breakfast – porridge – and stretch and visualise a bit.

Mum drops me into Belfield from our home in Whitechurch in Rathfarnham at 1pm as I still haven't learned how to drive. I've just turned 20 and I'm in my second year in the Academy, but my mode of transportation is a bike. And as most of the Academy sessions start at 7am in the David Lloyd Leisure centre in Riverview, on weekdays I usually have to be on my bike by 6.15am.

She then goes to have lunch at Brownes in Sandymount with her friends from work in Brabazon Nursing Home to celebrate her birthday two days earlier.

Throughout my school days in St Columba's, and all my games with various Leinster teams and the Irish Under-19s and Under-20s, she's never missed one in Dublin before, or that many outside Leinster either. I remember she didn't make it to a school game in Sligo once. But today she is coming back for the second half.

Dad and my brother Philip, who's living in Churchtown, are coming to the game separately. My uncle Ian and aunt Val McCulloch are also in the stand. It's just the three of us – me, Mum and Dad – in the family home as Andrew and Philip, and my sister Emma, have all moved out and on with their lives.

The weather is good for January and the pitch has always been one of the best in Ireland so you know it is going to be a good game. Lansdowne have Devin Toner, Dominic Ryan and Stephen Keogh, and we have John Cooney, and Rhys and Ciaran Ruddock, all of whom are in the Leinster and Irish underage and senior set-ups. Big players for a Division 2 game.

I'm playing at '12' today, inside-centre. I prefer '10' but Niall Earls is having a good season at out-half and I have been chopping and changing between the Leinster XV, the Leinster 'A' team and UCD.

WHY ME?

I'm happy to be playing rugby. Matchdays have long since been my favourite days.

With an hour and half until kick-off I am nice and calm. The warm-ups go smoothly, with no injuries, so we are all good to go. UCD have a big following, so there are a few hundred in the Belfield Bowl. Not thousands, but not just a man and a dog either.

The game kicks off and it starts like a top-of-the-table clash should do – fiery.

Inside the first five minutes we are attacking on Lansdowne's 10-metre line. John Cooney passes to Niall Earls and I take a crash ball off him. Next thing I'm on the ground at the bottom of a ruck and wrestling for possession. I go for one big rip as I am lying on my back. For the split second that I am in this position, something catches my face.

It is an almighty impact.

I do remember hearing my name being called out before the impact, and then my left eye going completely black, followed by a constant ringing in my ear. It felt like a boot striking straight down onto my face.

My eyeball has just burst.

I stand up and look for a fight. I'm raging. The first thing I see is the 6' 11" frame of Dev Toner. A little scuffle breaks out but nothing major. I am seriously pissed off though as I thought it was some Lansdowne prick trying to take me out.

I look to the sidelines, where the UCD doctor Tony McDowell is coming toward me.

3

He looks at me and says: "Ian, come to the side."

I know straight away it is pretty serious. I am told to lie on the ground and my face is covered. Dr McDowell calls for an ambulance as he has some expertise in eyes and appreciates the severity of the injury.

Philip has walked around the back part of the pitch towards the UCD dug-out. When he says he's my brother they rush him to my side. Philip would tell me subsequently that he'd never seen me so filled with rage.

But Philip acts very calmly, as if nothing serious has happened. My Dad, who came to the game in his own car, soon makes his way over too. They are asked who would like to come with me to the hospital and Philip volunteers, leaving his car in UCD.

Dad will follow us but not until he has spoken to some of the senior people in the club to find out what exactly happened.

The ambulance arrives and I am taken to St Vincent's Hospital to check if I have broken my cheekbone. Philip is with me in the ambulance and at this stage has texted Mum to say I have been taken off injured. Initially she isn't too worried as I have picked up a few injuries in my career. Torn ligaments. Shoulder and hip injuries. Broken wrists from playing Gaelic football.

Philip isn't an alarmist but when he then rings Mum, she knows that it is a bit more serious. It's not like Philip to ring. She leaves her lunch and comes straight to Vincent's. The UCD doctor comes to the hospital too.

When the ambulance arrives at St Vincent's I am taken straight through to the Accident & Emergency Department with Philip. I begin to realise how serious this might be. I'm still wearing all my UCD kit and boots, with a long, full UCD jacket to keep me warm.

Philip has his arm around me on my right-hand side as we walk through, passing the waiting area to my left. The clank, clank, clank of my studs on the hard hospital floor would have drawn attention but other patients stop what they are doing and look at me. Others walk by but turn their heads to keep looking at me as well.

I am immediately examined by a doctor. Things are a bit hazy at this point. I have a scan, very quickly, which reveals no fracture in my cheekbone. I don't know this at the time, but after looking at me, a doctor advises Philip to get me to the Royal Victoria Eye and Ear Hospital on Adelaide Road.

I find out later that he said to Philip: "He's lost his eye. It's gone."

Philip tries to stay calm, for my benefit. Mum calls to say she is near Vincent's and Philip asks her to meet us outside the A&E entrance.

Mum pulls up at the entrance to the A&E. She sees her son still wearing all his rugby kit, a patch over his eye and Philip beside me.

I sit in the front seat of the car and say: "I'll have a look now". Philip pleads with me not to look at it. "It won't serve any purpose," he says. Mum is concentrating on driving. I lift my patch down and all I can see is my eye is out of the socket and it's not really looking like an eye. I can't distinguish my eye colour or my pupil. It is all grey and white. It looks horrendous, like someone has wrapped layer upon layer of clingfilm over my eye. Mum later recalled my first reaction: "Ah sure, that will be like a black eye in the morning." I am blasé about it, probably not comprehending the gravity of the situation.

We arrive at the Royal Victoria Eye and Ear Hospital where the UCD doctor was in the car park and speaks briefly with mum. I go straight to the Accident and Emergency unit. A trainee doctor is on call and I really feel sorry for her. She takes one look and says: "I'll be back to you in a second."

In a very calm way she has gone to find someone with more experience. I am left on my own in a dark room for an hour at most, maybe 45 minutes, but it feels like an eternity. My mother would feel guilty about this subsequently but she wasn't to know I'd be left on my own for so long. No-one comes out to tell her to stay with her son. I feel very frightened for the first time, and vulnerable and lonely. I actually begin to cry.

A new doctor by the name of Dr Eugene Ng comes into the room with Mum. He looks far younger than his experience and professionalism quickly suggests.

From the second he starts talking I know that I am in good hands. He explains that something very serious has happened and that time is of the essence. No specific details are given to me but he stresses that we need to act on this very quickly. I am immediately whisked upstairs to the operating room where I am prepped for surgery, which lasts about four hours.

While I am in surgery, Dad drops Philip back to his car at around 9pm to a now deserted UCD. On their way back to UCD however, Dad receives a call from John McClean, UCD's then Director of Rugby. Dad pulls over to the Spar car park in Milltown where John tells him that what happened to me was an accident.

I've never seen the incident since and the only person who has ever seen the video is John McClean and we took him at his word.

Philip also informs Dad that I am probably going to lose my left eye. He'd later tell me that he'd never seen him so angry.

Mum, in the meantime, has briefly spoken with Dr McDowell before being brought to a recovery ward where I will be moved after the operation and where other patients are all lying in different recovery positions.

Halfway through the operation another surgeon is called in, Mr Billy Power. He is one of the top ophthalmologists in Europe and he tells my mum: "I have never seen anything like this."

Knowing me as well as I know myself, Mum immediately asks: "Will my son be able to play rugby again?"

His response was blunt: "No".

"Will he even be able to drive?" she asks, as I am about to take my test.

"Yes. People can drive with one eye."

But the picture being painted to her is fairly bleak.

Mum can't process all this terrible news but knows she just needs to be strong for her youngest child. When I come back in from surgery, to her surprise, I seem to be in good spirits. Despite the drugs, I'm pretty alert and hopeful things are going to be fine. This makes it harder for her to hold the tears back given what she has just been told, but she does.

Mum goes home for the night and has to relay everything to the rest of the family, to Dad and Philip, to my oldest brother Andrew, who is living in the north, and my sister Emma, who lives in Dundrum with her husband George.

I get some much-needed sleep before waking up at around 5am with an almighty hunger and thirst. I hadn't eaten food since midday before the game. I'm given the classic tea and toast combo. About 20 slices of toast, which feels like the nicest meal I've ever eaten. This is the only bright point in these two days.

Next morning I wake up and I am just looking for some clarification as to what actually happened.

My eye is very itchy, as if there is mud inside it and it has been played around with, but there's a patch over it, which is just as well. No specific details of the surgery have been given to me yet.

Mum, my girlfriend – and now wife – Cordelia, and her brother George, come in to visit this morning. George is still in boarding school in St Columba's and we were going to take him out for the day until all this happened. I first met Cordelia when I was 17 in St Columba's, in 2007, and we started dating three months before the Leaving Cert in 2008, so we've been going out with each other for almost two years now.

She's studying art history and history in UCD, and working in O'Brien's off-licence in Donnybrook, which is where she was on the day of the accident until 10pm.

I am in a general ward with six beds, but I am in good spirits.

Dad comes in later. Mum has asked him to bring in some toiletries for me. He can't find my toothbrush and toothpaste so he stops off at a pharmacy. But instead of toothpaste he buys dental removal gel and instead of an adult toothbrush, he buys one for a child.

"What's this?" asks my mum.

Dad's life is work and helping parishioners. That's his calling. And he's amazing at it.

We all have a badly needed laugh.

Dad then explains that John McClean had rung him the night before after studying the incident on video numerous times. McClean confirmed that it had been a boot with a light blue sock which had landed on my face.

UCD colours.

Thankfully it wasn't an opponent because otherwise things would have become a lot uglier.

Later that day I am wheeled into a private room where I begin my recovery.

My abiding memory is seeing Mr Power's name written above the headboard. I initially think this must be my nickname, because this is such a powerful injury.

Mr Power comes in and, using all his experience, explains in a very clear manner what has happened. I have sustained a serious injury.

"Your eyeball has perforated and we had to clear away a lot of matter that was unnecessary and unused," he says. "You have an eight millimetre gash at the top of your eyeball, which is where all the excess liquid came out. We had to stitch it up."

He says it is a very strange injury. He doesn't paint a really grim picture, or not to the same extent, as I learn later, as he does for Mum.

I don't ask about details. Maybe I don't want to know.

"When can I get back to playing rugby?" is my first reaction.

"This is a really serious injury," Mr Power says. "Let's just take it day by day."

• • • • •

I have always seen my rugby career as a fight to reach the summit of Mount Everest, clawing and punching and digging my way to the top.

Now I've been hit by an avalanche that I don't want to admit has happened. Now it's a case of how quickly I can get out from under this avalanche. In training you're always taught to get up off the ground as quickly as possible. Don't show weakness. It's like army training and this is my mentality. I'm grand. I'm going to get back. As quickly as possible.

So, I dutifully begin doing everything that is asked of me. I take my eye drops every 30 minutes through the first two days and nights. Then it's every hour. A nurse comes in and wakes me up to apply the drops. I also have to sleep in an upright position and not look at TV or mobile phone screens.

All that week in hospital I am shattered; from the surgery, from the constant care and eye drops I have to receive, and from being inundated with visitors. Everybody means well, and I appreciate every visitor, but I have to repeat the story over and over and over again.

My mum keeps saying: "If you're tired, just tell people." By around day four or five, sometimes I have to say: "Can I just have some time? I'm so tired."

Whenever I see a doctor they have to shine a particular type of sharp light into my eye, during which I have to keep my eye open for as long as possible. I feel my eyeball shaking because it's under so much pressure.

On about day three, I take a shower but I am under strict instructions not to get water on my face. It requires a big effort. When I eventually get home, Mum or Cordelia have to wash my hair. But I can't lean back or forward, which makes me feel very vulnerable.

I am humbled by the constant stream of visitors – all my family, all my friends, almost the entire UCD team and the entire Leinster squad and academy. Not just playing squads but staff, so 70 or more from each. People I hadn't seen in ages come in to see me. Hundreds of people. Literally hundreds. At times, they're sitting in the room and standing all the way out to the corridor in an orderly queue.

All day is visiting hour.

The only time I'm on my own is at night. I have almost no time to myself, so much so that if the security staff or receptionist or secretary sees some burly rugby types coming in through the front door they immediately nod to the first door on the left of ten rooms in the corridor and automatically say: "Room one."

John McClean calls into me with another UCD official on the Wednesday. What makes his version of events more concrete is that two days later the player concerned visits me. I know it's him. He acts sheepishly and asks how I am. We sidetrack the topic.

My mum is surprised at how calm and relaxed I am. But I believe I will be back, that this is a little bump on the road. I have more important things to think about, like recovering and playing again.

A hospital didn't seem like the right place to lose my head. Maybe I am also still in shock. But I don't want to hold any animosity toward him.

The teammate would later confirm he had been responsible in a fully apologetic letter to me, which took a huge amount of courage on his part. I wrote back to him saying there was no problem.

That week McClean told me that he couldn't believe how I had so little anger inside me.

But that anger will surface in time.

•••••

On Friday, Leo Cullen and Brian O'Driscoll come in before the Leinster squad fly to Heathrow for a European Cup game against London Irish in Twickenham the next day. I am amazed that they make time for me before travelling to London. Drico gives me a punnet of grapes.

When I tell Mum and show the grapes to her, she says: "Right, we're not to touch Drico's grapes!" This becomes a running joke. They bring them home and even leave them in the fridge for a few days before eating them. They are Brian O'Driscoll-bought grapes. They can't be hurried. They have to be savoured.

The next day Leinster draw 11-11 through a last-minute drop goal by Johnny Sexton, although I struggled to watch it because my eye hurt.

The nurses seem happy with the constant stream of rugby players calling in to see me.

We joke around with them. "Are you single? Are you in the market for a rugby player?"

Mum is given her own car parking spot. The whole staff are like a big family and they're fantastic, particularly Patricia Conn, the department secretary, a parishioner at Whitechurch.

All week she is brilliant in helping to arrange appointments with doctors and this special treatment continues in the coming weeks as I have appointments every two days.

Two days after the op, I can begin to see the outline of my mum with my left eye, which is fantastic. After another day or two I can begin to see light. Then I can begin to see letters, much to the amazement of Mr Power. This is a ridiculously good start. We aren't expecting to keep the eye, let alone for it to begin functioning again so soon.

That is all down to the talents of the medical team.

But then there are also moments which underline the scale of the damage. Depth perception, for example. Two days after the op I turn to a jug of water and glass on a table beside me to my left. I attempt to pour water into the glass and all I hear is water pouring onto the floor. My depth perception is so bad I miss the glass by about three feet. I can't distinguish how far or close the glass is from me.

Cordelia is with me when this happens. It's our one time on our own all week. 'What the hell is going on here?' I think. My mates at school would always say my hand-eye coordination was pretty good. You could put a tennis racquet in my hand. Or a hockey stick. Or a hurling stick. And no bother to me. To go from that to this?

But the light coming back is encouraging.

After a week in hospital, I am back home but with strict instructions. I still have to put these drops into my eye regularly, I still have to sleep in an upright position and I am not allowed to do any form of physical activity because my eye is so delicate. But I am home and I can now begin my recovery toward my obsession – getting back onto the rugby pitch.

TWO

Coming Home

I WAS released back to the family home in Whitechurch before lunchtime the following Saturday. That week in hospital had seemed like a month.

The nurses had been inserting the eye drops every hour so I never had a full night's sleep. The visits started at 9am and finished around 5pm. Everyone came with the best of intentions, and it was wonderful, but I'd grown weary of reliving the story.

Cordelia and I had one hour on our own throughout the entire week.

I was also tired of sharing one bathroom at the end of the corridor with the patients in the other nine rooms. I was tired of the hospital food. I was just tired.

My life would be repetitive and mundane for months to come. But at least I now had a purpose and a plan to regain some vision.

My left eye was still incredibly bloodshot but I could just about make out faint light, rather than pure black, which was miraculous according to Mr Power. That gave me hope too.

I still had to wear a patch, to make sure no dust or dirt came into contact with my eye. I also had to take three different types of drops at regular intervals every day. They were mainly for keeping out infections and they were applied by my mum, my sister or 'Cords', as I still found it quite hard to open my eye.

They would also set their alarm every two hours through the night to apply the drops. As time went on it became part of my routine and therefore easier. The dose gradually decreased to less regular intervals over the next few months.

I had to constantly clean my eye with a cotton bud as 'gunge' would develop around it. I didn't venture outside as daylight put a strain on both of my eyes and there was also the anxiety of something accidentally falling into my bad eye. Although I had the patch, there was always the fear of a rogue leaf follicle or something.

Apart from appointments with Mr Power, I didn't venture outside for the first month.

The day after the surgery I'd asked him: "When can I go back training again?"

He said: "Take it day-by-day. It really is a day-by-day scenario but I can't envisage you doing anything until next year."

Two days beforehand he had told my mum that he didn't think I was going to see again in my left eye, which shows how well the operation went. His initial priority was that I didn't lose the eye.

I was prepared to do everything by the book. My recovery was so important to regaining some vision, so I did everything Mr Power told me to do. But I wasn't prepared to agree with him on one thing. He'd said it would be a year before I could take any kind of exercise. I wasn't waiting a year.

I couldn't have done it without my mum, my sister and Cordelia. Even writing this makes me appreciate even more how much my mum did. Mum mothers us quite a lot, and as the baby of the family, me in particular. Probably too much. She probably still thinks of me as a toddler.

Like any good mother, Mum tried to keep up my spirits and do as much as she could for me. These months were tough for her. She felt fairly helpless emotionally so she decided to give me as much practical help as possible. Making sure I was clean, that I took my drops and made my appointments with Mr Power on time. It was her way of being there constantly.

Initially I didn't take a shower for fear of water getting in the eye. In that week in the Eye and Ear I'd had one body wash. When I came home, I had to have my mum, my sister or Cords wash my hair over the bath. I would sit on the bathroom floor and tilt my head back over the rim of the bath. I was even afraid to push too hard when going to the toilet as that might have put an extra strain on the eye. Honestly.

I couldn't bend over to brush my teeth or eat so I would have to sit at 90 degrees. My toothpaste, brush and a glass of water were on a shelf in my immediate line of vision. Likewise my food was propped up on a tray in front of me. I was not allowed to sleep face down or to the side, so I had a V-shaped pillow which made me sleep face up.

All this was tedious, but it was important to ensure the blood was flowing correctly to keep the eye functional. And with every visit, my eye improved a little, which was vindication for everything I was doing.

I couldn't put too much pressure or strain on the eye, so I didn't watch much television, didn't play much computer and didn't read that much. Laptops were around then but there were no iPads or anything like that, and that probably would have made it harder.

Worst of all though was the lack of any kind of exercise.

So this recovery was very different from other post-injury periods of recuperation. Normally you would have something you could work on. For example, if you have a leg injury you can work on your upper body strength. But I wasn't permitted to do anything. I was alone with my own thoughts a lot.

•••••

At first, my visits to the surgeon were every two days, and then after a couple of weeks every three days and so on, to once a week.

I looked forward to those checkups in the Eye and Ear. It was just a relief being able to go out of the house and do something. I would leave in the morning with Mum, and we would park outside the hospital on Adelaide Road. We were really well looked after by the secretary, Patricia Conn. She made us feel very at ease.

We would walk through the main entrance of the hospital where there is a striking staircase which loops around both ways to the first floor, where Mr Power's appointment room was located beside the operating theatres.

Mr Power would engage in conversation with Mum and there were light-hearted moments but he was dealing with me as I was, after all, an adult and the one going through it. Hence, he needed to be more matter of fact, which I actually preferred.

From the outset, Mr Power always stressed one thing: "We cannot have anything bad happen to your retina." That would be dangerous territory. He also guaranteed that when someone has a trauma like that to an eye they would subsequently develop a cataract, which would require further surgery, but he said we'd cross that bridge when we came to it.

My main memory of those initial visits was applying stinging eye drops for dilating the pupil. An incredibly sharp and painful light (via a prism) made my eyeball shake constantly.

While doing this, Mr Power would say: "Look left. Look up. Look down." It was like looking into the sun. I detested that part. The rest of the visits I didn't mind.

The most important thing however, every time I went back I

was increasingly able to make out the sharp hospital lights and shapes in the room, which was a miracle.

As my vision improved, Mr Power would also hold up his fingers and say: "How many fingers am I holding up here?" After about three months I could make out how many he was holding up.

Looking at the eye chart initially with my bad eye I wasn't able to make out the letters but, similarly, I gradually began to make them out as well. After a while I could read the first line, then after a while the second line and after about four months the third line. That was very exciting.

Even though Mr Power always preached caution, and although he didn't always say it, I could tell he was pleasantly surprised. But he still wasn't giving me any indication of when I could start training again. Baby steps. Whereas I wanted to sprint 100 metres, he wanted me to walk half a metre first and go from there.

A few weeks into my recovery, I visited the Leinster staff in their Portakabin area at the back of Riverview, just to keep them up to date and wish them luck for the rest of the season. They just had a gym and some offices there – basic stuff – which is hilarious when you think of the major European force they've become. I opened the coach's door and Michael Cheika came out from the corner and shouted: 'McKinley mate, where the fuck have you been?'

I had a very good relationship with Checks. He is a very

strong character, very Australian. I think he liked the way I played, a physical '10'. He capped me when I was 19 away to the Dragons in Newport. That was the week before the 2009 Heineken Cup final and with a weakened team, but it still had Sean O'Brien, Rob Kearney, Devin Toner, Girvan Dempsey and others. He must have seen something in me.

Typical of a rugby squad's culture, the whole tone when I called in that day to Riverview was quite jokey. I still had the patch over my eye and one member of staff shouted: "Hey, Popeye." Rugby banter. I wasn't sure whether to find that comical or be offended. I laughed it off, but it probably wasn't the best thing to say to a 20-year-old who has just had a severe eye injury. At this stage it wasn't clear whether I'd ever play again at all, never mind for Leinster.

As time went by though, I could begin to embrace a funny side to it all. I have quite a dry sense of humour and innocent phrases became a joke. Someone said to me: "Ian, will you keep an eye on that."

"Ah c'mon," I said back. "You can't be saying that to me. You can't be slagging the disabled." When I met up with some of Cordelia's mates, one of them had bought me a pirate's patch, which I happily wore over the actual patch. I was able to joke along because my eye was improving all the time.

Another early landmark, after two months, was being able to take off my eye patch.

Suddenly this meant I didn't get stared at so much in public and it gave me confidence to start doing things on my own again.

My brother, Philip, lived in a house near the Windy Arbour Luas station so I would be dropped off there by mum, hop on the Luas, get off at Charlemont and walk to the hospital. It was always a really nice walk along the canal.

After the checkup, I'd take the same route back and often call in to Philip. From there I could be picked up and brought home. I had started to drive a little before the accident, and one of the first things my mum asked Mr Power afterwards was whether I'd still be able to drive.

He said: "Yes, people with one eye can drive legally with no problem." So this meant I could study the theory, with a view to learning and getting my test.

Once I arrived at the outpatients, I would walk through the main waiting room and down a corridor where there were different consultants' names written above the door. I would sit outside and wait to be called. The corridor was so narrow that you had to keep your feet or you'd trip someone over.

While waiting, all I could hear were the many different accents from people who had obviously travelled far for their appointments. The majority seemed to come from Cork, Kerry, Mayo, Donegal or wherever, so I felt lucky, and even guilty, given my short trip from Rathfarnham.

When I went into Mr Power's room, there was invariably another consultant there with another patient. Trainees were always flanking Mr Power as well, watching his every move. I think my case was a particularly interesting one for them, so at his invitation they would take turns to have a closer inspection of me. I didn't find this invasive. It actually made me feel, in some weird way, a little special and that Mr Power was giving me the most of his time. Even though I wasn't a child, he was making a little bit of a fuss over me.

But my vision kept improving, and my appointments with Mr Power became weekly.

After about four months of this routine and four months of asking the same question of "When can I go back?" Mr Power eventually said there was now no reason why I couldn't do some light stuff, although we were still in this six month danger zone so it came down to my confidence.

I wasn't allowed to push too hard or run too fast just in case I went too hard too quickly. It was almost going into the unknown for Leinster, Mr Power and myself in terms of a training schedule. I started back with Dan Tobin, one of Leinster's Strength & Conditioning coaches, who would give me small exercises.

I could go to the gym, but I couldn't lift anything heavy. It was almost like a yoga class. Slow, methodical movements. A restart session, basically, with your body. I did the bench press with just the bar, which is 20 kilos. Push-ups on Swiss balls, just to ensure stability and comfort. You lose a lot of fitness and muscle in four months without doing anything.

But to be doing even such basics was wonderful for my mental state.

•••••

I had booked a holiday with some of my rugby mates from the academy and the Irish underage set up. I was humming and hawing about it. Mum and Dad were both of the same opinion: "Go. You've got the green light from the doctor to fly. You've had a horrendous time. Enjoy a holiday with your friends."

A group of us went to Sunny Beach in Bulgaria for two weeks, which was probably about ten days too long, but it was nice not having to think about my eye for the first time in five months. Peter O'Mahony, Jack McGrath, Ciaran Ruddock, Eamonn Sheridan, who was with Leinster as well at the time, Peter Synnott, who had won the Leinster Schools Senior Cup with Belvo, and Shane Ronan-Duggan, a friend of one of the lads, were on the trip, as was Ian Madigan.

Mads and I chatted freely about resuming our battle in Leinster's out-half pecking order. "May the best man win," we agreed. He'd overtaken me but I vowed to him that we'd continue our on-field rivalry.

We had known each other since we were nine, through playing Gaelic football at Kilmacud Crokes. The first time I met Mads was in a car on the way to play Lucan Sarsfields with our coach, Gerry Greene, and his son David. Although he was a year above me in school, we had been contemporaries all the way up the underage rugby ranks, him coming through Blackrock and me at St Columba's.

I had about 50 percent vision back in my left eye at this stage, but I was ready to get back into the full swing of things. When I did it was straight into 2010-11 pre-season training with Leinster that June, less than six months after the accident.

The speed with which I had returned surprised the doctors but looking back, I don't think I'd fully prepared myself. If this was to happen now I'd have a much longer run-in to full contact.

My first training session was a rucking drill run by the forwards coach Jonno Gibbs on the UCD back pitches. I took a big deep breath and just cleaned out a player – I'm pretty sure it was Nathan Hines holding the pad or else it was him taking the ball into the pad and I cleared the ruck.

I stood up and thought: 'Okay, I'm grand.' And that set me on my way. No comment was really made about the eye which was fine by me.

This was also Joe Schmidt's first year as Leinster coach.

My first impressions? He was a very impressive figure.

He had come from Auckland Blues and then three years at Clermont as backs' coach. Although he'd met Brian O'Driscoll and Leo Cullen before taking the job, he was unknown to most of us. He was slight in stature but commanded respect.

Checks had transformed Leinster but immediately you could just tell that this guy was bringing us onto a different stratosphere. Training was so intense on the detail. Everybody talks about it but it was just so true. We trained on the far pitches in UCD. We would all hop into each other's cars from Riverview and the coaches would drive their vans over.

Physically, it wasn't too hard. Anything but, actually. But mentally it was exhausting.

With Checks, we would beat the shit out of each other. I even dreaded some of the academy pre-season sessions. In one we played six-a-side on a full Gaelic pitch in UCD with a 5kg medicine ball!

Friday was usually the day when you did all your aerobic/ physical training. But the rest of the week was so specific on skills drills and moves. Getting basics and details right. Physically I thought it was almost too easy but Joe made me think of things that previously had never crossed my mind.

Joe usually made us do a passing exercise where we had to pass in order of the number sequence he called, which was to trigger our brain. There would be five of us in a line and he'd go: "One, two, three, four, five." And we had to pass the ball in that sequence. Then he'd go: "Five, four, three, two, one." Then he'd mix up the numbers completely and you'd have to pass in that sequence really quickly. If you got it wrong he'd give you an absolute bollicking. Fear went through you doing that drill. And we always did a ten-minute passing bloc at the start of training.

He wanted to make us the best passing team in Europe.

I would have struggled with my left-to-right passing. So I knew that if I was ever to play for Leinster under Joe I would have to sort that out. There were a few other guys whose passing should have been better than it was and he just constantly hounded you at it.

He was also ruthless, utterly ruthless. At team meetings, if you didn't know everything about your opposite man you weren't playing.

As a head coach, he had a point to prove as well. He was so intense, but he wanted to be the best and so we needed to get things absolutely right on the training ground first. He was the boss, but sometimes with the backs he would make us come up with a play to get to a wide area, which made us all think. Although it's changing now, most coaches told you what to do, but Joe tried to put some responsibility on us as players and I think he was a little shocked with the moves we devised. I don't think he was too impressed with what we had come up with.

We usually had a big training blow out on the Friday, and I remember playing games that I had never seen before which not only challenged everyone aerobically but also mentally. Isa Nacewa was usually brilliant at all of them. I'd say if you asked Joe who was the best player he ever coached it would be Isa.

There was one particular game called 'Fiji Touch' which essentially was touch but the player in possession had to be touched by two opponents for him to be turned over. It might sound simple but Isa would often stay on the wing, run at the one person opposing him and then score a try.

Whether he knew the game beforehand from training with

Joe in Auckland I don't know but Isa was the first person to invariably crack any of these 'games' Joe devised. Isa was able to problem solve very quickly and had all the skills to match.

Isa initially arrived as an out-half, but ended up playing mostly on the wing or full-back, which was just as well. Otherwise between himself and Johnny Sexton, the rest of us would never have had a look in.

I did spend a good amount of time with Johnny, as this was my third season in the academy and I was in and out of training with the senior squad, and also when we did kicking sessions with Richie Murphy. You could tell Johnny was still riding the crest of a wave. He'd been waiting but his opportunity had come a few seasons before and now he was grabbing it with everything he had.

I played outside him at '13' in a training game at the RDS. I had played '13' before but only occasionally. I called for the ball but I didn't call for it loud enough, and he gave me a bollicking. One of the coaches came up to me a day later and told me: "Ian, if you want to play for this team you have to start talking." I was a bit pissed off that Johnny didn't come to me rather than the coaches. But it made me realise you have to be the general, the conductor, at '10'. You have to be a dominant figure, to have people around you do the right things.

Although he was another in opposition, the Australian out-half Shaun Berne was a great help to me in the way he did the basics and remained calm. He talked you through training and when he was at '12', for a young out-half, he was good to play with too. He made the game simple and clear, and you can see now why he has gone on to become a coach because he was a very intelligent player and had a very composed way about him.

Isaac Boss was also very good to me. On one occasion when I got something wrong Joe lambasted me and I felt horrible afterwards. Isaac came past me and whispered: "It's a good thing he's shouting at you because it means he cares about you. If he didn't he wouldn't say anything to you." I would learn the truth of that years later. Better for a coach to be shouting at you than ignoring you.

Overall though, pre-season training went pretty well and some of the lads went out of their way to say I looked pretty sharp which gave me a huge lift. I was doing loop plays a lot, which with the depth perception wasn't the easiest, but otherwise it all felt natural, like before.

Joe was as animated for a pre-season friendly as he would be for a European Cup final. He wanted to ensure everyone was on the same page, challenging each other.

• • • • •

My first game since that fateful day at the UCD Bowl was a pre-season friendly the following August against Wasps in Donnybrook which featured the seasoned internationals Phil Vickery and Serge Betsen in the starting line-up. There was an interesting dynamic on the bench as Simon Shaw was 36 and would soon become the oldest player to ever play in the Six Nations, while there was also one of the youngest ever players for Wasps, Elliot Daly who was just 17 at the time. I still had 50 percent vision in the eye but I felt fine. I was itching to make up for lost time. We lost 41-6 in front of a crowd of 5,640, which was really disappointing considering the team we had out.

I got the last 25 minutes at out-half and I didn't defend off a midfield scrum as Joe wanted me to do, 3/3, with three players on each side of the scrum, but we did a 4/2. Joe Simpson scored for them and I was at fault.

Joe gave me a right telling off the following Monday. It was one of the most in depth reviews of a game that I had ever experienced and this was a pre-season game. It lasted about an hour.

At times in the game, Joe highlighted players from the other side of the pitch who didn't chase hard enough. Monday reviews were pretty brutal, and you needed a thick skin. Coaches and players were very honest with each other but this was how it had to be to get the best out of the team. It also definitely marked an attitude shift among us.

A week later I started our last pre-season game against Leicester at Welford Road. The Leicester team was captained by Irishman Geordan Murphy and also featured the former Munster out-half, Jeremy Staunton who replaced Toby Flood after 50 minutes. The legendary Italian tighthead prop, Martin

Castrogiovanni and English scrum-half, Ben Youngs also started. The first-half went pretty well. Near the half-hour mark, we had a penalty advantage 30 metres from their line. I chipped and chased over the New Zealander Scott Hamilton, got a lucky bounce and re-gathered. My first try for Leinster.

However, I was brought back to earth soon after when Leicester brought Alesana Tuilagi in off the wing to first receiver for an attacking scrum. I tackled him but he still ran over me for a first phase try. Not a pleasant experience. To make matters worse his younger brother Manu Tuilagi, then 19 years old, played the second half on the other wing.

Bizarrely, nine years later, I would end up having to mark Manu for 50 minutes at outside centre in Twickenham during the Six Nations. Leicester eventually pulled away in the second-half to win 37-14 but I thought it was a better team performance than the previous week.

I also thought I'd done enough to start the following week. But Joe told me I only passed the ball five times in the 50 minutes I played. "Macker, why didn't you have the ball in your hands more often?" he asked.

I said something along the lines of the forwards had been going well and I thought it best to play more through them. But he wanted his '10' to be much more involved. Bottom line: I hadn't had the ball in my hands enough.

But if a coach is honest with you that's fair enough. At least he gave me a reason rather than no reason. And I certainly wasn't getting any special treatment after my eye injury. Nobody made mention of it whatsoever and I was happy about that. I was treated like any other player and that's all I ever wanted.

Besides, from lying on that hospital bed less than eight months beforehand to this point, it had been a pretty good comeback, but at the time I just wanted to be starting for Leinster.

Nonetheless, a week later in our first Magners League game away to Glasgow, Isa started at '10' with Mads on the bench. And that was the way until Johnny came back into the team after his later start to pre-season.

So for me it was back to the AIL where I needed to rebuild my game with new teammates and a new club.

I had decided to move from UCD to St Mary's RFC for two reasons. One: I didn't want to play with the teammate who stood on my face. Two: I wanted to play at the highest level of club rugby that I could, and that was with St Mary's.

They were in Division 1A and UCD were in Division 2, two tiers below. UCD had been relegated at the end of the 2008-09 season in a last-day shoot-out at Belfield against Young Munster. With two minutes to go it was 14-all and a draw would have kept us up and sent them down. I hit a 22 metre restart to half-way, close to the touchline. Their winger caught it, passed it to Mike Prendergast and, boom, his drop goal from a metre inside their half sailed over.

But it was time to move on from UCD. During my pre-season with Leinster I called in to John McClean, the UCD director of rugby, in his office. First I told him that I had been given the green light to play again.

"This is great. We can start planning the season," he said.

He was ecstatic until I outlined my reasons for wanting to move club. His expression completely changed. He was annoyed and held my registration for a little bit, longer than I wanted. But I asked him to understand my circumstances, which were a bit different from anyone else.

I said: "You surely don't want me playing with the guy who did this?"

I didn't meet him again but after a few phone calls he eventually released my transfer form. At the time of writing John is facing numerous charges of indecently assaulting former Terenure College pupils. However, during my dealings with John I was unaware of any claims about him.

I was still living in Whitechurch and St Mary's was only a ten-minute drive away. Ciaran and Rhys Ruddock had also moved there from UCD. So instead of being in Glasgow with Leinster, I played my first game with St Mary's in a friendly away from home. I came on for the second half and played pretty well. I linked up nicely with the '12' Mark Sexton. He's the brother of Johnny and Jerry, and now coaching with Ireland Under-20s and Connacht.

In the last few minutes they made a break down the wing. I tracked across and tackled their winger. A ruck later we conceded a penalty. One of their players tapped and went quickly but I held him back, which pissed him off. I knew exactly what I was doing, and a minor scuffle broke out. Nothing too major. Then out of nowhere, from behind me, one of their players put his hand over my face and dug his finger into my good right eye.

I shouted: "Get the fuck away from my eye." Some of my teammates saw this and Mark pulled the nutcase off me.

Some of the lads said: "Do you not know what happened to this lad?"

His response was: "Yeah, I know what happened to him. I broke my leg last year and you don't hear me complaining about it!"

I didn't know what to say. I was in disbelief. So I just walked away and finished the game. I chatted to an old schoolmate of mine who was playing for the opposition.

"What is up with your man?" I asked him.

He just said that the lad was a bit of a loose cannon.

There were no cameras there or video evidence. It was his word against mine. So I didn't file any complaint. I told my parents and Cordelia. They were all irate. But what could I do? It was done. Finished.

In another game at Templeville Road, in January 2011, fingers were dug into my eye at a ruck with that classic backward motion. I let out a scream. It was sore. Hugh Hogan, the captain, went to the referee and said: "'Do you know what this guy has gone through?"

The ref said: "I didn't see anything so there's nothing I can do."

Again, there was nothing I could do either.

I had a really frustrating time at Mary's on the pitch but off the pitch it was, and still is, a great club. Shaun McCarthy, a talented Australian out-half, had been there a while and I found it hard to get picked ahead of him. I felt I never got a fair go. I started a few games and subbed a few games, some at '15', and I was so desperate for some game time at '10' that I played a Junior 1 game one Sunday.

Word must have reached Joe that I played a J1 game on a Sunday at out-half because he said to me that having versatility is really important. In other words, I was better served playing at '15' for the Mary's firsts than at '10' for their seconds.

But I'd had a career-threatening injury, I wanted to make the most of my time as a player and I believed that '10' was where I would perform best for my team.

We missed out on a play-off spot on the last day when we lost away to Old Belvedere, ironically my best and last game for Mary's, and at '10', thanks to a wonderful individual try from their number 8 Leo Auva'a, who played for Leinster a few times.

I also played seven games in the British & Irish Cup for the Leinster As, although we didn't exactly live up to our nickname of 'The Assassins'. It was the second year of the competition. In our first game we won 33-28 away to Newport in October, with Mads at '10' and me at '12'.

In December we played Plymouth on a Friday night in Skerries only for a power cut to put the lights out after 20 minutes. It must have been a sign from up above, because I was having a shocker.

The game was played the following afternoon in Greystones, when I had a good game, and we won 25-16.

I was on the bench away to the Cornish Pirates in December. Men v Boys. Horrendous performance. We lost 43-12. We flew back late that night to an empty Dublin airport where, to our surprise, the first team were waiting for us at the arrivals area – and were all dressed up for their Christmas party in fancy dress. That was surreal. One particular teammate, Tom Sexton (a social hero) was asked out by the first team and duly obliged. They picked up a few other stragglers who wanted to go out with them, but most of us took the bus back to Riverview.

The 38-23 win away to Worcester in January was a good one. I started, we had a good team out and so did they. A week later, we won again, 30-7, away to Currie RFC, in January, although I was subbed for Mads, who needed game time. You're never happy when you're taken off, especially at half-time.

But the quarter-final away to Bedford in March was shambolic. Malcolm O'Kelly was our team manager and he had to come out of retirement because we were so short on locks. It's hard to imagine that situation happening now.

I was captain for the second half but this was an embarrassment, especially as Joe had flown with us to watch the game.

Everyone gave up with around a quarter of the game

remaining and we lost 50-15. We had good players and you're trying to force your way into the senior squad. One of the most depressing games I've ever experienced. I remember Collie McEntee, who was our academy manager and the 'A' team coach, coming up to me and saying: "At least you didn't give up."

It wasn't good.

By then, I'd played my first competitive game for Leinster in 15 months against Aironi in February in 2011 – my first time togging out in the RDS too and with all my family there. It was only 12 minutes but it couldn't have gone any better. When Joe brought me on the game was in the balance. I felt really comfortable and embraced the occasion. The game was tight enough until a 78th minute try by Dave Kearney after a great Shane Jennings offload in the corner.

On the Monday, Joe told me: "With the game being so tight it shows I have faith in you." That gave me some confidence.

A week later I started away to Cardiff. It was a very flat performance. We were on the ropes for most of the night. Ceri Sweeney in particular showed me how to run a game that day and I wasn't happy with how I controlled it.

I defended well and stopped a couple of tries. I put in a good hit on ex-All Black Xavier Rush but Joe would have been unhappy that we even got ourselves into that position. Subbed after 50 minutes. If I was dropped I wouldn't have had any issues but I was picked to start again a week later at home to Benetton.

This was it.

I was in the third and last year in the academy. Deep down, although nobody said it to me, I was playing for my first professional contract. Some of the senior players might renew in December, but for the young guys, February is your last chance to get your foot in the door.

I was playing for my future with the province. I felt confident, and picked up a try and an assist. Joe had said during the week that Benetton were pretty weak around the fringes.

Dominic Ryan, aka 'Dippy', was having his breakthrough season and ran at their first pillar defender to make a break from our own 22. Off quick ball, Bossy passed to me and I passed it to Isa. He put rip-roaring speed on to it as he does and offloaded to Dave Kearney, and he passed to me. I stepped their Italian centre, Ezio Galon, and finished from about 45 metres.

Afterwards, I was presented with the Man of the Match award on the pitch, an engraved iPod and headphones. A ridiculously nice prize. I had my photograph taken and saluted my folks in the crowd. 'Wow,' I thought, 'I've done well.'

But as I walked into the changing room with my prize, Joe was lambasting people. He was unhappy we didn't get the bonus point. As a performance, it wasn't good enough. I walked very sheepishly over to my spot. That changed my attitude towards how you review a victory and team sport. Joe was always expecting more.

After Joe left the changing room, Isa asked me: "Macker, what did you get?"

"Well, I'll show you."

He was like: "Fuck, far out! I've got Man of the Match in the last few games and I've just gotten Nivea products. You picked a good day to get Man of the Match!"

Looking back on what later transpired with my comeback, this match proved to be deeply significant.

To play in the number 10 shirt of Leinster at home in the RDS, against what would become my future club, Treviso, and to score a try and receive Man of the Match after my injury, marked a really momentous day in my career. Indeed, Leinster v Treviso fixtures in the RDS would come to mark a whole series of milestones for me over the next number of years in a variety of different ways.

• • • • •

I played one more match for Leinster against Glasgow in May. I came on at '12' for the last 25 minutes at the RDS and played okay but the game was already won. I think Joe saw me as a viable option at '12', which may have got me into more matchday squads, as opposed to a specialist's '10'.

That month I was awarded my first senior contract.

Two weeks later I was part of the non-playing contingent that was flown out to Cardiff for the 2011 Heineken Cup final. The Johnny-inspired comeback against Northampton.

After full-time, initially we weren't allowed onto the pitch but eventually we were. We each held the trophy, took part in the lap of honour and went into the changing room. I can't speak for anyone else but I felt a little out of place.

I was registered for the Champions Cup and I trained all season with the squad but I didn't play in any of the European games. I'll cherish the medal but I felt I hadn't earned it, although it made you want to be a part of something like this in the future.

When leaving the Millennium Stadium we walked through the crowd to get the bus back to the airport and I bumped into my cousin, Ross, who put his arm around me and shouted: "We fucking did it." Clearly, like many others, he had been drinking since that morning but the sight of him and then another Leinster supporter celebrating halfway up a lamppost were funny moments.

Cardiff Airport was full of supporters. You could barely move. There were two scheduled Leinster flights. The first was for the wives, girlfriends and families, and us non-playing squad members, and the second for the team and the trophy.

The dinner and celebrations were in the Burlington Hotel, now the Clayton. I left around 2 or 3am as a few of us had to play a game for the Leinster As against the Irish Under-20s in Wanderers relatively early the next day in preparation for their Junior World Championship campaign.

The next morning, Wanderers was eerily quiet compared with the Millennium. I was up against Paddy Jackson. We started well, I slotted a penalty and then we scored a try. As I was lining up the conversation at the clubhouse end, I looked up at the posts. They were really fuzzy.

I said to our physio: "Something isn't right. I need to come off."

I somehow landed the conversion but took myself off as my vision was deteriorating. I showered and called Mr Power. He'd always said that if I ever had any concerns, or if my vision deteriorated in any way, to ring him. He wanted me to call in the next day and said: "It sounds like a cataract but I need to get a better look at you."

The next day in the Royal Victoria Eye and Ear, Mr Power confirmed I had developed a cataract. He had said that a cataract could happen at any time, be it in five or fifty years. In the event, this was 14 months, and it required surgery.

Normally a cataract surgery is 15 minutes long and requires a local anaesthetic but because of my previous history the surgery had to be done under general anaesthetic and it lasted about 90 minutes. Afterwards I was sent home, where I had to have more drops applied.

Normally, after an operation on a cataract, you would take off your patch after a few hours and be able to see clearly again. But my vision was still blurred in my left eye. It wasn't improving. In fact it was getting worse and I could tell Mr Power was a bit frustrated with it. He said that I had a lot of blood towards the back of the eye. The surgery had been successful in removing the cataract but a couple of weeks later I had to undergo another operation to try and remove all the blood that would not go away, and which contributed to my vision being blurry.

I went into Mr Power for pre-op. He had to mark either side of my pupil with a tiny microscopic poker. He warned me that this would burn, and boy did it. That was acutely painful. When the accident happened, I was not in a huge amount of pain but when he singed my eyeball with a hot poker, I was in complete agony.

I could actually smell rotten flesh, which was very off-putting. I had the 90-minute operation under general anaesthetic, and went back home for recovery again, with more drops and more steroids to remove the blood. The blood in the back of my eye, along with the cataract, was causing the blurred vision. And the steroids made me extremely hungry.

A few weeks went by and my vision wasn't improving. I was really frustrated. Everything had been going so well. I'd been getting used to playing with 70 percent vision in my left eye. My confidence was back. The new 2011-12 season wasn't far away, and I hadn't been able to do any proper training.

One of my closest mates, Stewart Maguire, had moved to Connacht from Leinster. I was scheduled to go on a couple of trips abroad with him but I couldn't fly because of these surgeries. Instead I went to Galway with Rhys and Ciaran Ruddock to stay with 'Stew' as we knew lots of the lads he was living with.

This turned into a nightmare weekend.

Stew had to go to hospital as his appendix burst, Rhys picked up glandular fever and my retina became detached. Ciaran was driving and we stopped at traffic lights in Galway on our way back from seeing Stew in hospital. I was in the back seat, and when I looked up at the traffic lights I couldn't make out the colours. I knew I was in deep trouble.

I rang Mum and told her I was coming home early the next day. With two sick people in the car, Ciaran drove us back to Dublin. En route I rang Mum again to tell her that I thought something serious had happened. Mum drove me straight to the Eye and Ear, where Mr Power had referred me to another retina specialist.

After an examination, I was told immediately that my retina had detached. FUCK! This was what myself and Mr Power had feared.

I needed an emergency operation straight away and I was scheduled to recover in hospital for a week.

For the previous operations I was put under anaesthetic and on a trolley. This time I walked into the theatre and was flanked by nurses before being put under anaesthetic. This was my fourth operation and the most important one.

•••••

When I woke up that night, back in a private room, I was very sore but in good spirits. Cordelia was working that night. Mum and dad came in to see me. They were told to expect me to be lying face down on the bed for a couple of days as this was the common position after a procedure like that. I was sitting up though, which alarmed them.

The surgeon asked to speak to my mum and dad in the corridor. He told them that working with my retina was like working with tissue paper due to the trauma my eye had endured.

And that the surgery was unsuccessful.

The surgeon told my parents he was deeply sorry that he couldn't save the vision in my left eye. He also knew that this would be devastating for Mr Power, who was away at that time, as he was highly invested in my case.

My parents were distraught but were told not to tell me anything because I was in post-op. The news had to wait until the next day. They came back into the room and Mum couldn't speak. I asked what was said. Dad kept it generalised so as not to alarm me. So they went home with all this information.

The next morning, Mum and Dad arrived first, followed by a good friend from St Columba's, Adam Philpot. He was a couple of years older than me in school, but I looked up to him because he was pretty good at rugby, which was unusual in St Columba's.

Adam had no idea what was going on but, of course, Mum and Dad did.

My whole world was about to be shattered.

Dr Eugene Ng, who was the very first surgeon I had seen from the initial accident, came into the room. He sat at the end of my bed and started explaining what my parents had been told by the specialist. As he was just beginning, Cordelia, Emma and George came into the room carrying some coffee and croissants. They were no doubt thinking, 'This is great, Ian is getting repaired again'.

Dr Ng continued and said: "We cannot save the vision in your eye as the tear is three times bigger than what we can repair."

My heart sank! I said: "What do you mean you can't save it?"

Dr Ng confirmed the eyesight in my left eye couldn't be saved.

Everyone in the room started crying. I looked straight ahead of me where I saw Adam with his head bowed and with tears rolling down his cheek. I felt so sorry for him because that must have been a hard situation for him.

I was sitting in bed with my knees up to my chin. I just put my head between my legs and started crying. I was comforted by Cords and Mum, but no one could say anything to make this situation better.

Dr Ng had left the room to give us some time together. I said to the nurses: "Is there any point in me staying? Can I go?"

So they went away to ask, returned and said I could go home.

I had gone into the hospital with dreams and aspirations of making a full recovery only to be told I would be blind in my left eye forever. I left with Emma, George, and Cordelia to be dropped back to Whitechurch. I left the hospital in such a rush that I forgot to take my medication, so someone had to go back to the Eye and Ear.

I don't remember much of what happened when I got home. But my mum recalls me going out to the back garden where I used to play any sport, mainly rugby, on my own. Where I first dreamed of playing for Ireland at the age of five. I stood with my back to everyone and didn't move. I didn't say anything.

I came back in. I wasn't crying any more. Mum, Dad and Cordelia all felt helpless. I then rang my big brother, Andrew, who lived up north, to tell him the news. But I couldn't speak. I started crying again. I eventually told him and we both started balling.

I then went up with Cordelia to my best mate Andy Lawler, whose house is five minutes up the road in Ticknock Road. Cordelia had told him what had happened. As I walked in the door I started crying again. They all hugged me as I broke down in front of the whole family.

Life was going to be different!

Whether I should have returned to playing rugby so soon, whether I should have gone to Galway that weekend, whether this or that, whether it was destined to happen anyway, I don't think Mr Power or any surgeon can know. All I know is that it happened.

The vision went black.

I was still on Leinster's emailing list. Even though I knew I would have to retire, less than a week after the operation on my retina, on July 21st, I went into Riverview. All the senior Leinster squad were having their head shots taken for the

2011-12 season. What was to have been my first as a proper professional.

I'm not really sure why I did that. In the picture, it's clear my eye is a bit wonky. Some of the guys said I looked pretty banged up. I could tell they felt a little sorry for me. Maybe I was still clinging to the faint idea that I could still be a professional rugby player. Maybe it was a last defiant gesture. Maybe I just wanted to be photographed in a Leinster jersey as a member of the pro squad. But I just wanted to do that photoshoot.

I tried to come to terms with my new life for a few weeks. I went to London for a few days as I needed to get away. I talked repeatedly with Dad. My options weren't great. Dad simplified the situation. Get a pen and paper, write down the reasons to keep going and the reasons to stop. If the negatives outweigh the positives the decision was made for me.

There were positives. I love rugby. I was born to play rugby. There was a vanity aspect – fame, glory, money.

But the negatives were more compelling. The pain in my eye was incredibly sore. Playing rugby, with the depth perception, would be quite difficult. And then there was the potential for gouging, which could have implications for my long-term health. I wasn't going to play rugby again without eye protection. I felt that would be stupid.

Yes, I thought, I'd done it before so I could do it again. But no matter what way I turned, or what spin I put on it, those three negatives wouldn't go away.

So that was that.

I was retiring from rugby at the age of 21.

I worked with Peter Breen, the Leinster press officer, on the press release confirming my retirement. On August 31st, 2011, I was waiting in my bedroom for the release to come out. I opened my laptop to play football manager, hoping that would take my mind off things and then, at midday, I received a notification showing the article that I had already read a few times over, entitled: "Ian McKinley announces his retirement."

My heart sank and I went completely numb. I knew it was coming but I couldn't believe what was in front of me. It was a very surreal moment. I knew then that mulling over a sad situation could lead me down a dark path, so I quickly came to the realisation that I had to keep active or at least find a change of scenery.

A few weeks before my announcement I called in to Joe Schmidt's office during Leinster's pre-season to inform him of my decision. I wanted to cry in front of him, but I couldn't. It was fairly matter of fact. He was sorry for me, thanked me and wished me the best of luck in life.

That's professional sport. That's the industry. I hadn't been looking forward to doing it and I didn't take my time. In truth, I hadn't fully come to terms with my retirement at all.

That would come a year and a half later.

THREE

The Son Of A Preacher Man

I WAS born on 4th December 1989 at Rotunda Hospital at 6.48pm. I grew up in Whitechurch in the Rathfarnham area of Dublin wedged between two golf courses, The Grange and Edmondstown, at the foothills of the Dublin/Wicklow mountains. I was also reared in a Church of Ireland rectory.

My dad, Horace, was originally from Templemore in Tipperary. He was a member of the clergy with the Church of Ireland, a Dublin Diocesan curate in Taney and then Rector of Whitechurch. His late father was Rector of Templemore Parish & Archdeacon of Cashel and Emly for many years. Even though Dad has lived most of his life in Dublin, he thinks Tipperary is the greatest place on Earth. He loves it.

My Dad's late half-brother was initially ordained for ministry in Waterford Diocese but then moved to England, where his lengthy ministry there included being Vicar of Hackney, in London's East End. My brother Philip has recently become a deacon and he's the eighth McKinley in our family tree to become a Church of Ireland clergy member. It's in the blood.

The only grandparent I never met, and Mum never met him either, was my dad's Dad, George McKinley. My grandfather was nicknamed 'The Revie' and married twice, hence why I have a half-uncle, Richard, who died in World War Two in the Battle of Monte Cassino at the age of 25. So his burial grave is in the Cassino War Cemetery between Naples and Rome.

My grandfather's first wife, Marion Hanan, sadly died at quite a young age and there were three children, Betty, Richard and Henry, from that marriage. His second wife, Marie, was the much younger Principal of St Mary's N.S., Templemore, and there was a considerable age gap between them. They, too, had three children, of whom Dad is the youngest. I just called Marie 'Gran'.

Dad's full name is actually Arthur Horace Nelson McKinley. He went from St Mary's N.S. Templemore to board in Portora Royal School, Enniskillen where Oscar Wilde and Samuel Beckett were educated and which is now Enniskillen Royal Grammar School. After finishing there, Dad went to Trinity College, Dublin, where he studied theology at the then Divinity School. It was while he was a young curate in Taney Parish that he met my Mum, Pam. They were married when he was 27 and she was 20.

Mum's full name is Irene Pamela McCulloch. She hailed from Churchtown in Dublin and attended Alexandra College, which was in Earlsfort Terrace in Dublin and not Milltown in those days. She then went to Taney and Whitechurch with Dad, and is now back living in Churchtown.

Her parents were Betty and Walter. My granny was born in Port Talbot in Wales, to Irish parents and lived most of her life in Ireland, and my grandad grew up in Arklow in Co Wicklow but lived most of his life in Dublin. He fought in the Second World War and then worked in insurance. His two big passions in life were gardening and playing golf, so with all the nice little golf courses around the area, Churchtown was perfect for him. My granny, who I called 'Mimi', worked in the same insurance company as my grandad and they used to attend a lot of dances together. She fell madly in love with him and didn't want to let him go.

My Dad was out of the house all day, every day, working long hours. He was also serving as a Canon of St Patrick's Cathedral, Dublin, which necessitated him giving time to it as well. Sunday was his 'rest day', when he would have taken three services, and that's not joking. You rarely saw him although he would always make the most important events.

So Mum was a stay-at-home mother until I became a little older, and then she moved into nursing home care at Brabazon House in Sandymount, where she worked for 15 years.

My family has strong roots in rugby. My grandad on my

Mum's side played in two Leinster Schools Senior Cup finals with Wesley College against Blackrock in the 1930s, both of which they lost.

Dad was a hooker with Trinity and Old Wesley in Dublin, two of the oldest clubs in Ireland, and also played for the Irish Universities. In the year when Mum and Dad were married, Dad was captain of Old Wesley RFC and Mum was captain of Old Alexandra Hockey Club. Their wedding photo featured in the newspapers alongside a caption about their joint sporting status.

He had, apparently, a bit of a reputation for being a hard player, I think partly because he wore a collar off the pitch so people thought he would be this nice gentleman on it. But I suppose if you were a hooker, especially back in the '60s or '70s, you wouldn't have lasted long as a nice gentleman. I think he was just the same as anyone else. We have newspaper articles of him at home from his playing days and he was captain of pretty good Trinity and Old Wesley teams, where he played alongside Phil Orr, a prop for Ireland and the British & Irish Lions.

I think Dad had a bit of country grit about him, let's put it that way from what I believe, never having seen him play.

Mum was a talented hockey player and loved it, but by her own admission didn't like training.

In their own different ways Mum and Dad have been pillars of support. Anything you need they've always been there for us and very loving. Mum would have been the more hands on, classical Irish mammy – washing your clothes and getting the dinner out – whereas Dad was always providing a house and going out to work and paying the bills.

Dad made sure you were in bed at the right time but as there was such an age gap between me and my siblings I think he certainly mellowed as time went on. Mum was the more cuddly parent but both were very effective in creating a really happy childhood for all four of us.

My older brother Andrew, sister Emma and younger brother Philip were all watching 'Home And Away' one evening when Dad called them into the kitchen to tell them that Mummy was expecting another baby.

Andrew was 14, Emma 12 and Philip nine, and this news promoted three very different reactions. Andrew was thrilled. He burst into tears and hugged mum. Emma was coy and Philip was very put out at not being the baby anymore.

Andrew and Emma were in St Columba's at the time. One day, a few months later, Andrew woke up to get ready for school. He went into our parents' bedroom, but no one was there. He went downstairs to be met by Dad coming through the front door. Mum had been brought in to hospital. I was born that evening, December 4th 1989, which was regarded as an early Christmas present for the family. An unexpected one too, given the nine-year age gap between me and my siblings. Hence I was given the title "the clerical error".

I came from a solid family which provided pillars of support. I was a novelty because there were no other babies at that stage in our family circle and effectively had five parents. Emma picked me up and looked after me as if I was hers. I was constantly dressed like a girl or a doll by Emma and my cousin Claire. I didn't have my hair cut until I was two, so I had long curly hair down past my shoulders.

Andrew has told me that a 'bouncer' was attached to the door, and I would be in it for hours. He knew from an early age that I had good coordination, even though he moved to Northern Ireland when I was three years old.

Emma has also told me that it was obvious I was sporty and athletic from a young age. Our grandparents had a net in their back garden in Churchtown, and my grandad would mark lines the old-fashioned way to make a tennis court on the grass in the summer. I beat Emma in a game of tennis there when I was eight and she was 20, and she maintains she was really trying.

Emma took me to Trinity, national galleries, and the national history museums regularly. She used to read to me most nights, mainly Roald Dahl books.

When she went to games, she noticed generally how most of the players were well supported by their mainly middle-class families. My kit had to be washed. I had to be driven to games and I needed to be fed well, which all was helped if you came from a strong background, so I was very fortunate.

Emma travelled abroad a fair bit, and she would always bring back exotic sweets that weren't around in Ireland, a 12-foot long bubblegum being a favourite.

Philip, initially, was very jealous of me and he even tied me up with a rope on the couch when I was three days old!

He would play pranks on me like pretending it was morning and telling me to get ready for school when it was still the middle of the night.

But of course we soon became very close. We shared a room for many years and would have good conversations before nodding off to sleep.

Philip was also my first sporting hero.

Along with Mum, I always went to his school games. He was a big centre, captain of the St Columba's Senior Cup team and played for the Leinster "A" schools, which was made of the smaller rugby schools, for two years.

•••••

For us, parish life was different from most kids' childhoods I'm sure.

Whereas now there are parish halls for the local community, when we were growing up our house was the parish hall. Sports days, committee meetings, bake sales all revolved around the house and the garden.

We constantly had visitors, be it Vestry meetings, Bible groups, various school related meetings, and worried parishioners or strangers coming to visit Dad.

The phone was always ringing. When Dad would come home from work, the phone would ring straight away. The running joke in the house was: 'Who is this stranger coming back and forth?' But he was just so dedicated to his work. I'm aware from about the year 2000 onwards, he also had to take on a significant leadership role in the Diocese, relating to programmes and initiatives of welcome and support of new immigrants to the city. This was known as the "Discovery Ministry".

Our house was always buzzing; people looking for help, looking for direction in faith, money or trying to reach out to people. Local meetings were held in the house and you could hear everything. If I was having dinner, I'd make sure not to disturb the local parishioners by going into the kitchen with my plate!

The Archbishop's name was Walton Empey and I used to call him 'Walto!' and rub his hair. It probably wasn't the most respectful way to treat an archbishop, but he didn't seem to mind.

We were very privileged to grow up in a middle-class family. It was quite isolated living there too. When Dad took over the parish in the '70s it was just fields and he was given five years to make something of it. In the 45 years he was there he re-opened the Parish school in 1978 and oversaw the building of a new school in 1990, and this has had two subsequent extensions.

There has been huge housing development around the whole country and certainly this is true of Whitechurch. So, he's made it into a thriving parish, as it has greatly expanded since he first went there. It was a picturesque place to grow up, at the foothills of the Dublin/Wicklow mountains. We were virtually tucked away from civilisation but yet if you chose your moment and if it was off peak traffic hours, you could drive into the city centre in 15 minutes. It was a great place to grow up and live.

In secondary school, from the age of 13, I went to St Columba's, which is a Church of Ireland school. There were daily church services and assemblies, and as we also attended St Columba's on Saturdays, the last thing I wanted on my Sunday off was another service.

I could play rugby and other sports during the week and on Saturdays in school, but my problem was that mini rugby in clubs is invariably played on Sundays, and on Sunday in our family you went to church. You didn't play sport.

Our service was at 10.30am every Sunday and my mum also sang in the choir. Dad would wake me up at 10am and off we walked up the road. It was normal for me and our family. It was normal to see Dad wearing robes and taking a service, or praying at the family table or praying with each of us. Dad would always say prayers with me before I went to bed.

I couldn't wait to get to Sunday school, if it was on, or go home after the main service as I found it all quite boring.

Coffee afterwards at home was then followed by a parishioner, or parishioners, coming to our house for lunch or a cup of tea. If I didn't have Sunday school, I usually played on the computer or watched GAA or Formula 1 at home.

I attended church every Sunday until I was 18, when Dad let

me go in my own direction in discovering faith and practising it. In fact, all four children have very different beliefs and attitudes to practising faith, and Philip has been ordained as a deacon.

My mum is from a Presbyterian background – she is a relaxed person – and has a sense of humour, even in church. Maybe not the classic rector's wife! She married into it very young. I think the balance they helped to achieve is amazing, to have four kids with such varying viewpoints. They can get a different fix from us all. For example, rugby from me or God and church from Philip. Conversations can go in any direction at home.

My brother went to Uganda and had a different experience for living his life the way he wants. That was for him.

Do I believe in God? I'm not as sure. I believe in something. Well, I want to believe there is something afterwards. What is believing in God? That goes in different ways. Is it doing the right thing? I am all for that. Is it to be a practising worshipper? That's not me.

Later in my life, after I moved out and then on to Italy, I only attended church when visiting my parents. But I learned to love hearing Dad preach. He's recently retired now after 51 years of service. I was maybe too young to appreciate what Dad was preaching about in his sermons but now I understand there was a fair amount of wisdom in what he said, the value of life skills and living your life in what he says.

Dad encouraged me to attend church on Sundays, but not in an overbearing way, while Mum was more relaxed, but the older I became the less I attended, until I stopped going altogether. It wasn't a conscious decision. I'm not an atheist. I'm not a complete non-believer. I believe the values of God can enhance everyday living. I'd still like to think of myself as a Christian, especially given my family background. Just a non-church attending Christian.

My primary school was Whitechurch National School, literally across the road from the Rectory, and a 40 metre walk from our house. So there were no excuses for ever being late. It is a Church of Ireland school that Dad played a strong role in helping to build. They even held a sport school day in our back garden.

Beside our garden was a Moravian Cemetery, i.e. with men on one side and women on the other. It was normal for people to ask for permission to walk through the garden in order to visit the graveyard.

Whitechurch National School is a beautiful school that, spearheaded by Dad, was built in 1990, and I might have received "special treatment" from teachers as Dad was effectively their boss.

There were around 150 pupils in the school so class sizes were small enough. Every Friday Dad would take assembly, give a reflection of the day and we sang songs like: "If I were a butterfly."

When I was in Senior Infants, aged five, the-then coach of Old Wesley RFC enrolled his son aged four for one year into

Junior Infants, one class below me. The dad, Mark Anscombe, would later become Ulster and Canada coach and his son Gareth went on to have great success as a Welsh international, receiving the Man of the Match award when Wales beat Ireland to win the Grand Slam in 2019. He also kicked the winning conversion in 2022 to seal Wales' first ever away victory over South Africa.

I played against Gareth in the Six Nations and marked him a good few times in the Pro12/14 where he played for the Cardiff Blues. It was interesting that a small school in the foothills of the Dublin mountains can lay claim to two coterminous kicking rugby internationals, one New Zealand born, who played for Wales and the other Irish born who played for Italy.

Every Monday, from the age of seven, I went swimming with the school in Templeogue College. My treat was always to stop off and get a pack of scampi fries on the way home.

I started hockey aged seven or eight when we would train and play out of Three Rock Rovers hockey club up the road. I was really excited when we started the games in our chequered blue and white jerseys. As a form of hydration, I just remember parents giving us segments of oranges at half-time.

My first memory of watching a rugby match was Ireland against England in the 1995 Five Nations. Ireland lost 20-8 at Lansdowne Road. I was five. And I was hooked.

A parishioner would always call over to watch the game with Mum and Dad, and I can still remember being enthralled by what I was watching. Mum usually screamed at the TV whereas Dad, despite having played rugby himself for many years, was very reserved and always stayed quiet. Even in years to come if Philip or myself were playing in games they were at, that was always the case. Dad never opened his mouth. I think that's because he knew what was going on. I'm more like Dad now.

That match sparked something. Straight after it I played my first imaginary Ireland-England game, although I had to use a round ball. About two or three years later though I had my first rugby ball, a signed Irish Gilbert ball which Dad won in a raffle.

We had a large back garden which was plenty big enough for a young kid to run out and play with a ball. Golf balls flew into our garden from Grange Golf Club regularly. I'd usually pick up about five balls a week, so there were always a few to spare.

I was always in the garden.

I'd often change into oversized rugby kit and boots. Then I would walk from my bedroom down the stairs and wait in the kitchen before running out in front of the 'crowd'. In my mind there was always a great atmosphere, and I would get to meet the president, sing the national anthem, and usually end up beating England. As I grew up in the '90s, when England usually beat Ireland, this fantasy grew.

During primary school, my first live sporting event was a League of Ireland football game – Shelbourne v Sligo Rovers at Tolka Park. I was brought to the game with my friend Conor Boyd by his dad Cyril and I also went to St Pat's and Bohs' games.

THE SON OF A PREACHER MAN

My English 'team' is Charlton Athletic. Back in 2000, 2001, everyone supported Man U or Chelsea or Liverpool but I didn't like the bigger teams. Charlton were going pretty well under Alan Curbishley and they had two Irish midfielders, Mark Kinsella and Matt Holland, and Dean Kiely in goal.

The first rugby teams I supported were Leinster and the Connemara All Blacks.

Our holidays were always in Connemara, usually me and Philip and Mum and Dad, and eventually just me and Mum and Dad. We invariably stayed in The Long House, on the coast road between Clifden and Roundstone. We played touch rugby with other families from Dublin who were on holidays in Connemara at Bunowen beach. Parents v children.

As we went on holidays to Connemara for years, we ended up supporting the Connemara All Blacks. The club is named after a type of fishing fly called the Connemara Black and the home pitch has a great name, Monastery Field. I wore their jersey growing up in my younger years.

I was 12 when they made it to the All-Ireland League Division 3 final in 2002 against Trinity in Lansdowne Road, the first ever time Connemara made it to the home of Irish rugby. They won 25-21 in an historic victory. Cult heroes like Gerry King and Frank Madden were fan favourites of ours, although Philip claims my love of tough rugby players has dwindled since I moved to a Mediterranean lifestyle.

By then I'd also been to Lansdowne Road two years

beforehand for the 2000 Celtic League final with Philip and our good friend Charlie Langley, when Leinster beat Munster. Philip took me to other matches too, like the Belvedere College v Blackrock College schools cup final in 2005.

Phil and I also played plenty of rugby in the garden together and, of course, he toughened me up. Sometimes I complained to Mum and Dad that he would be too rough, like when shaking me out of a tree. As I was falling I caught my thumb on a branch and broke it.

We would also play rugby in the hall. Phil would usually win. He was on his knees, and I would always run into him. We would also box each other using our Grandad's boxing gloves from World War Two.

Philip is very musical, and we would write songs together, but as I am tone-deaf, I wasn't much of a sounding board.

I was lucky that I didn't have many distractions from playing sport. Philip recalls that I went through a bad PlayStation phase. I'd play for hours and when he walked into the kitchen I would be whacking the side of our tiny TV, which had a crack down the middle of the screen, with my hand, to make it work.

In sixth class, I went to a week-long rugby camp in St Mary's RFC and picked up 'the star player award', a little more confirmation for Mum and Dad that I wasn't too bad.

Yet they insisted I went to St Columba's. Other parents would say to my parents: 'Why would you send him to St Columba's when he is so sporty?'

Mum would say: "There are other things in life besides sport." She felt my education should be rounded.

Yet Mum would be my biggest supporter in the years to come. She worked at Brabazon House Nursing Home in Sandymount until 2pm most days, and our games usually started at 2.30.

In any case, following in my siblings' footsteps, I began attending St Columba's College aged 12 in 2002. It was the closest school to our home. It was generally a boarding school but because we lived so close, I went as a day pupil.

St Columba's seemed to suit me. I was happy there, made some lifelong friends and the school supported me in everything.

Every day started with chapel at 8.15am and I was normally home at 6pm. Half day on a Wednesday finished at 4.30pm and there was the dreaded Saturday school from 8.50am to 4.30pm.

The school was compared to Harry Potter because we had to wear these traditional black gowns and then white surplices on saint days. Sometimes pupils would come down in their gowns to watch our games, which was a bit cringy.

St Columba's was quite intimidating at the start, especially in finding your way around due to the size of the campus and the names of classrooms which weren't your average 'Room 1' or 'Room 2'.

I studied a rich variety of subjects; Latin, Classical studies, French... but all I could think of was: 'When can I get out onto the pitch?' Any pitch. Any sport.

St Columba's was famous for producing politicians who

served on both sides of the border, a variety of artists, including painters, writers, poets and U2's Adam Clayton and Victoria Smurfit among others.

Rugby, hockey and cricket are the main team sports, and there's also athletics, tennis and basketball. For GAA I went elsewhere.

•••••

I can distinctly remember being in the car with Mum when we drove by Ballyboden St Enda's GAA Club (My Dad interestingly had been elected an honorary vice president with the neighbouring Ballyboden Wanderers GAA Club for years) or past Broadford Rovers FC and I would always say the same thing to her: "I just want to be out there with all those other kids".

In 1999, it was then suggested to my mum by her friend Alison Boyd (Fraser) that I could take up GAA with Kilmacud Crokes in Stillorgan. I was really friendly with Alison's son Conor and the idea was that we would play together but if I had been born three weeks later I would have been in the younger category. Thankfully this didn't happen, as the team was the most successful in Crokes' underage history.

I turned up for training in Deerpark in Stillorgan in grey school socks and although I had watched some Gaelic football, I didn't know some of the rules. But I loved it.

Whenever the ball came to me I just ran with it, never bouncing the ball or 'soloing' with it. I kept getting called back for 'travelling'. I eventually caught on! My first game was against Sarsfields in Lucan. The coach, Gerry Greene, drove three of us in his car; his son David, Ian Madigan and myself.

We won something like 15-11 to 1-2. The majority of our goals came from the ball bouncing in front of their keeper and over him into the net. The phrase "let the ball do the work" became synonymous with our training sessions. We lost only two games in five years. We won everything, but it didn't count for anything unless we won the Féile.

Not really growing up in a GAA background, I didn't know what this was, but I learned that it was the most important Under-14 tournament in Ireland. Qualification kicked off first in the counties, so we were playing out of Dublin. The event was held in Ballyboden GAA Club, and we played against teams such as Na Fianna, Cuala and St Vincents. We won all our games to eventually become the highest ranked team in Dublin for the All Ireland Féile Peil na nÓg in 2003.

A few weeks prior to the All-Ireland event, I tore part of my quad muscle just kicking a ball in training and you wouldn't haven't gotten better service from a professional team. I was seen straight away by a physio where I was told exactly what to do. I wasn't exactly 100 percent for the tournament but was pretty close.

The All-Ireland event took place in Galway, where there was an opening ceremony with a marching band in the magnificent Pearse Stadium. Each team was presented and had to march onto the pitch, division by division. There were five divisions in total.

My family was in the crowd, but my brother Philip hadn't arrived yet. Timekeeping would not be his strong point. Next thing, we hear the announcer introducing the teams and who do we see marching in the middle with the teams with a backpack on his back but my brother Philip. My family had a giggle as he made his way to his seat.

We were based in Claregalway who we played first. I was rooming with Barry O'Rourke, our star player, so I remember being really nervous around him because he was that good, but we got on well. The games were different as they were only 15 minutes a side, so you really had to start well. We played teams like Errigal Ciaran (Tyrone) and Corofin (Galway) along the way to us getting to the final.

The final was played against Castlebar Mitchels (Mayo) in Pearse Stadium in Salthill, a near 30,000 capacity stadium. My family recall, as we were warming up for the final, the announcer in the stadium was going through the previous results of the finals and in division five the Aran Islands had beaten New York. My Dad just thought that this was fantastic. "Where else in the world would get a final like that?"

We were trailing badly early on 2-2 to 0-0. I didn't have many wow moments like some of the other lads, but I do remember two things. I played a one-two and kicked a point from 40 metres out on the angle which helped generate momentum as it was our first score. In another incident, their full forward was one-on-one with our keeper. I managed to chase back and dislodge the ball, and eventually we won. I am proud of my All-Ireland club medal. It's rare for a Protestant to have one!

Our squad was: James Mulvaney, Oran Turley, Robert O'Loughlin, Rory O'Carroll, Ronan Walsh, Ian McKinley, Ronan Byrne, Karl Dias, Cillian McCaffrey, Barry O'Rourke, Ian Madigan, William McEvoy, Shane McNicholas, Conor Allen and Ciaran O'Grady.

In 2004 we followed this up with an Under-15 provincial championship win over St Vincents in Parnell Park but then I had to take a break from the GAA as I couldn't commit to the training and games due to Saturday school.

But I still occasionally played with Kilmacud Crokes and even played for the Dublin Under-16 teams, against Longford, Wicklow and Meath. But I then reached decision time. Rugby or GAA. And I had decided I wanted to be a professional rugby player.

My report cards were always the same; polite kid, could apply himself a lot more in class but a wonderful sportsman. My first taste of proper rugby happened in first year when we went to Kings Hospital to play a 10-a-side, Under-13 tournament.

The Junior Cup Team (Under-15) coach, Alan Cox, was there and suggested to Mum that I play on his team, but we thought it best to just keep going in first year. But in the following two years I did play on the JCT, winning and captaining our junior cup team to the Duff Cup (a competition for smaller schools) in 2005. It was the first time St Columba's had won the Duff Cup in many years. We beat St Pat's Navan, captained by future Irish Under-20 teammate Eamonn Sheridan, 6-3 in the final at St Mary's RFC in Templeville Road. The goal was to get to the main schools draw but we lost to Roscrea.

When I was a teenager and began climbing the rugby ladder, the family became really excited. Emma has told me it was particularly exciting going to my games as I was becoming known and articles were being written about me. She says it was brilliant as a family member to live it and be a part of it.

At the start of fourth year (2005), I was picked for the Leinster "A" school's side, which is drawn from schools who played in the A section of the Leinster Schools Senior Cup, to play Connacht and Munster 'A'. It was an Under-18 team and I was still only 15. This was my first taste of interprovincial rugby. We lost against Connacht but had a good win over Munster on the main pitch in Donnybrook; the first time I had ever played there.

I had to shower quickly afterwards and go with my family to the RTÉ studios up the road in Montrose as my brother, Philip, in recognition of all his work for unaccompanied minors in Ireland, was going to be featured on a show called 'When Dreams Come True', hosted by Ray D'Arcy.

Philip went to the RTÉ studio thinking the show was being done for someone else. As a further surprise the family was invited to come on set from backstage, and we all congratulated him for his achievements. As I shook his hand, he was highly embarrassed at this stage. Yet he pulled me a little closer and whispered in my ear: "Well done today". This was his moment, and he hadn't been at the game, but it typified how selfless a person he is, and that moment has always stayed with me.

•••••

In my fifth year in St Columba's I was playing in a hockey game in Bandon, Cork. I was normally the player to lead the defence charge to block a short corner as I was quick. I sprinted out, like I normally did, but the opposition player sliced his shot and the ball cannoned straight into my patella.

There were no doctors or physios there, so I just limped off unable to continue. Later that night after the game we were staying in the dorms on site. As we were heading to bed, I was in plenty of pain and the master in charge scraped ice from the freezer into a flannel, and applied it to my knee. It didn't help as whatever ice was gathered had melted immediately!

This incident led to patella issues which kept me out of rugby for about ten months. I missed an Irish School's trial and a Leinster Schools tour to South Africa as a consequence.

The layoff actually afforded me more time to focus on what I wanted to do and that was to be a professional rugby player. In that summer of 2007 I rehabbed every day and decided to drop the hockey and the Gaelic football to concentrate solely on rugby. I even turned down a Leinster hockey trial.

That summer Richie Murphy, now the Irish Under-20s head coach, ran training sessions with Leinster underage players who hadn't been picked for South Africa in Terenure College. I loved them. I felt the best I ever felt, and I was training really well. There was talk of me being added to the squad for South Africa but it had already been picked.

This annoyed me as I felt it had something to do with attending a smaller rugby playing rugby school. It made me even more determined to prove people wrong.

Instead, I was selected for a Leinster Under-19 squad which was coached by Dan van Zyl, where training was also in Terenure College. When I arrived, I realised I was the only one still in school.

These were players I'd watched in schools cup finals previously and an Under-20 World Cup so now I was stepping up to a whole new level.

The games were at Greystones RFC. I played one warm-up match and three interpro games, at '10', '12' and '13'. We won one and lost two, but the coaches said to me after the last game that I was their player of the tournament, which gave me a massive boost going into my last school year.

I started my last school year as captain and we began strongly, winning all our games well. This was really important because I wanted to put St Columba's on the map and show that we were a decent team.

I also started my third year with the Leinster "A" Schools,

but I was called up to the main Leinster Under-19 Schools team which was a goal I had set before the season began. It annoyed me when we had to wear our school socks to trials as I felt there was a preconceived idea of you based on your school, so to make the squad convinced me I was picked on merit.

In a warm-up against Bedford Academy in Bedford I was on the bench and was given the second half to show what I could do. I played well and was selected for the interpros. We won all three games, beating Munster on the back pitch in Donnybrook, Connacht in Athlone, and Ulster in Dungannon. I played '13' for the first two but was at out-half against Ulster. That was probably the best game I played throughout my school career. Everything went right and my confidence was sky-high. It was a good day for St Columba's because my teammate from school, Chris Lilly, was with the Under-18s team, which was pretty unheard of for any small rugby playing school. Again, after the tournament, I was told by the coaches that I was the standout player.

With St Columba's, we won the McMullan Senior Cup (third division) but our goal was to reach the main draw of the cup. We upset CUS in the Vinnie Murray (second division play-off) which earned us a first round match in the main draw. Unfortunately, we were drawn against CBC Monkstown who were favourites for the whole thing, but we honestly thought we could win. The size difference between the teams was ridiculous. They had players in the back row at 6' 5" and 110kg.

Two of our flankers were no bigger than 5' 9" and 85kg so it was a mammoth task. Thank God for the max 'one metre push' rule in the scrum or it would have been carnage.

It was the first time in a long time that St Columba's had made it this far, so we had a huge amount of support. St Columba's had, it's true, won the Leinster Schools Senior Cup once before, beating Blackrock in the final. But that was in 1899.

CBC led 3-0 at half-time and we genuinely thought we could do this, but size and power won out and we tired, eventually losing 24-0. Still, I couldn't have been prouder of everyone. To this day it remains one of my proudest rugby playing memories. We had a few "quiet ones" in Johnny Foxes that night.

In March 2008, I was called up to the Irish Under-19 squad, a combined youth and school team, for games against Italy and France. This was my first experience of international rugby. Allen Clarke was head of the IRFU performance unit and Under-20s coach for the following year and I think my performance against France left an impression. He shadowed us a fair bit and towards the end of the school year, I was selected for the IRFU Academy, and we trained out in DCU.

The IRFU Academy was a selection of players that were highlighted as "probables" to go on and play for Ireland at senior level, but as we know this is never a guarantee.

After those Under-19 games I also received a letter to attend a meeting for entry into the Leinster Academy. This was it, the critical next step toward being a professional rugby player. I could only think of this and not my final schools exams, the Leaving Cert.

Two months before the Leaving Cert, I also started seeing Cordelia. It probably wasn't ideal timing with the exams coming up, but I just needed a decent score in biology and maths and I'd be happy enough. I worked hard for the maths result I needed though.

The interview day came for entry into the Leinster academy, and my parents were invited as well. It took place in the old Berkeley Court Hotel and I was interviewed by Leinster chairman Frank Sowman, academy director Collie McEntee and CEO Mick Dawson. My first job interview.

Mum and Dad were explained the outline of the academy programme and warned that things might, or might not, work out for individuals. The panel emphasised to us that things sometimes don't work out for players so it was important to continue studying in addition to training. My parents would have been aware of this.

A few weeks later a letter arrived in the post addressed to me with the Leinster crest in the top corner. I had been accepted and would be officially registered in the Leinster academy the day after my Leaving Cert. I was one of three players that year to go from school directly into the Academy.

I was on my way.

FOUR

Living The Dream

THE ONLY rugby player prior to me who is listed among the St Columba's alumni on their Wikipedia page is Harry Read, who represented Ireland at rugby, cricket and tennis before the First World War, and subsequently became president of the IRFU in 1955.

My dream was to become the second Irish rugby international from St Columba's, and in June 2008, after the last exam for the Leaving Cert, I went out into Dublin city centre with my friends to celebrate the end of our school years together.

The night you finish your secondary schooling with friends you've known for six or more years is traditionally a big one. For almost everyone involved, tomorrow doesn't exist. Getting hammered is the name of the game. But I didn't taste a drop of alcohol that night. I slipped home, without so much as a goodbye to anyone, relatively early.

Although I wasn't starting in the Leinster academy for another few weeks, I was lacking technically in the gym, and I had arranged to go in on my own to work with the club's Dan Tobin.

I'd undergone physical tests beforehand, as this advance programme had been planned out with Dan, who'd previously worked with the Dublin senior football team and would go on to work with the Leinster squad before joining Gloucester.

The conditioning work was everything I wanted it to be in terms of intensity and accuracy. The thought that there were people there trying to make you the best you could be made me more excited. Every time Mum picked me up, I was just buzzing at the thought of going back the next day. I was in my happy place.

I lacked size and I lacked technique in the gym. Dan helped me hugely in a short space of time. When the academy started up, we continued to work on a one-on-one basis every morning before official training began. I put on about 6kg in a month, so the effort was worth it.

Collie McEntee and Richie Murphy were our coaches. I loved working with Richie as he was a fellow left-footed out-half. There aren't too many of us.

I also loved training with players like Felix Jones and Niall Morris for the first time, players who I would have seen a fair bit on television with Irish underage teams. I looked up to them. Of course, I looked up to Brian O'Driscoll, Felipe Contepomi, Rocky Elsom, Isa Nacewa and all the rest of them even more and, in the academy, we trained with the senior Leinster team as well as amongst ourselves. So this was a different level for me altogether. I was learning from the very best. I was jumping from the third tier of schools' rugby in Leinster to training with one of the top teams in Europe. That was quite a leap.

There was also an Ireland National Academy, overseen by Allen Clarke.

In the summer of 2008 the National Academy was seen as a platform for elite players from the four provincial Academies to have extra training in Dublin City University. It wasn't a team playing in a league. There was a presentation for the parents explaining what it hoped to achieve. I remember they put your name up relative to your position, so there were names like O'Gara, Sexton, Keatley ahead of me in the out-half category but that was the target to reach, and even surpass, one day. I don't know why but after a couple of camps it didn't continue. Maybe a congested calendar.

When training finished on one of those days, I hopped on the number 16 bus from DCU on the north side of the city centre across town to St Columba's to find out my Leaving Cert results.

My best mate, Andy, waited all day to get the results with me. He was aiming high whereas I just needed those two good grades, in biology and maths. He opened his results and he was really disappointed. I opened mine and I was ecstatic as I thought I had more than enough for my first choice, a diploma in Sports Management in UCD, but I was reminded that I had to drop one subject score for the actual result. Laughter filled the room at my expense. Ultimately though, I was accepted into UCD for the Sports Management Diploma.

I had a 15-week pre-season. Sessions were gruelling. Two, in particular, were horrendous; 15 rounds of three-minute boxing sessions taken by Michael Cheika and a game of touch rugby, six players versus six, with a 5kg medicine ball.

The final three rounds of the boxing session involved a 'Royal Rumble' style set-up which was essentially a free-for-all in a very small space, with up to 20 of us in total. You had no option but to throw punches at anybody you could reach, as long as they were not headshots – everything had to be from the neck down. One day Felix Jones caught me from behind with a kidney shot and the wind was completely taken out of my sails. I fell to the ground and Cheika shouted: "Get the fuck up mate". He was trying to make this club toughen up.

Collie McEntee ran the touch rugby session on a GAA pitch in UCD which was 140 metres x 90 metres. It was full on. We also did a few double gym sessions during the week to add bulk, which focused on plyometric work, in other words being explosive.

At that stage in my life I still hadn't learned how to drive. Hence, I'd cycle from Whitechurch to Riverview and back.

Sessions started at 7am so I would leave the house at 6.15am. We always started with gym before the senior lads came in.

Once finished, we would sometimes get shepherd's pie or lasagne for breakfast, which was tough to stomach at 8am or 8.30am.

For lunch you would have to prepare something yourself the night before. I usually went to the local Applegreen garage around the corner or sometimes I'd piggyback on what the seniors were provided with. Nowadays, most clubs would have built-in restaurants and regular chefs for all dietary requirements.

Then we'd walk through the Riverview back pitch and onto the training pitches in UCD.

Sometimes I'd finish at the same time as Mum, when she worked in the nursing home in Sandymount. She'd pick me up from the Dropping Well pub in Milltown and we'd stick the bike into the boot. When I did cycle home, it took me about 45 minutes as it was all uphill.

If there was a bigger break during training, I would hang out with the lads or go to my aunt and uncle's house in Churchtown for a nap to recover. This was not the norm for most 18-year-olds just out of school and embarking upon a new life in college, but I was happy. I was doing what I wanted more than anything else in the world.

I trained with the Leinster Under-20s mainly in Donnybrook. We won the interprovincial title, winning all our games. I started at '10' in each of them. I made my Leinster "A" debut in a friendly against Bristol, who had, of all people, the former Irish international Kevin Maggs at inside centre. A tough man to tackle coming down my '10' channel. Made of pure muscle. I was 18, he was 36 – twice my age.

A couple of weeks before the 2009 Heineken Cup final in May, 2009, I was at home when Mum answered the phone and said to me: "It's for you." It was someone who claimed to be, and sounded like, Michael Cheika, telling me I would be starting my first game for Leinster against the Dragons at Rodney Parade the week before the final. I genuinely thought it was a teammate impersonating Cheiks at first before realising it was actually him. It was one of the happiest moments of my life.

•••••

At the start of the week, before the squad flew to Wales, there was a meeting between the team leaders, assistant coaches and Cheika in the upper offices of Riverview to plan how we were going to beat the Dragons. Everything was just really exciting. I roomed with Rob Kearney, and he was coming back from injury, so this was a big opportunity for him to stake a claim for the matchday squad the following week. I believe, at the time, I was the fourth or fifth youngest to be capped at senior level by Leinster. Girvan Dempsey, Devin Toner and Sean O'Brien were also in the team.

I played 70 minutes, the result wasn't good (we lost 18-9),

but I was satisfied personally with my own performance. After the game someone asked me for my autograph, which was a first.

Toward the end of my time in school, I had been approached by about six clubs in Leinster to play for them. I chose UCD because I knew their Under-20s team was traditionally strong, the scholarship would help me with my studies and, conveniently, it was right beside Leinster's training base.

Lectures for my diploma in Sports Management only took place on Mondays, and UCD wanted me to dedicate that day to attending lectures. They made Leinster aware that I could train the rest of the week but just not on Monday. That started off fine and I would normally be in the gym for 7am and then the lecture hall at 9am. But, gradually, I was called up for senior training either late morning or in the afternoon so I would skip my lectures to train.

I found myself in a tug of war, but I knew if Cheika wanted you for training, then you made sure you were there. Once you got your foot in the door you had to keep it there.

In all I played a total of 49 games in that 2008-09 season with six different teams, the UCD Under-20s, the UCD senior team, the Leinster Under-20s, the Leinster "A", and the Leinster and Ireland Under-20s.

At UCD we had a strong Under-20s side, which made my time there very enjoyable. At the end of the season I won the young player of the year award, which I was very proud of because there were some exceptional players on our team like John Cooney, Shane Grannell and Noel Reid.

I was told it was relatively unusual for a UCD Under-20s player to be promoted to the seniors in a player's first year, but after UCD lost the Colours match to Trinity on November 14th, 2008, I was called up to the firsts. They were coached by Bobby Byrne and ex-Ireland international Killian Keane. I played my first senior rugby game aged 18 in an All-Ireland Cup game against Rainey Old Boys, the team I now coach. I was playing at '13' that day.

A couple of weeks later, on December 5th, 2008, I started at out-half in the All-Ireland League at the Belfield Bowl against Ballymena. John Cooney was also called up to the bench for his first taste of senior rugby. That team had Kevin McLaughlin and Fergus McFadden, both of whom would play for Leinster and Ireland, and the winger Vasily Artemyev, who went on to play for Blackrock and would also captain Russia at the 2019 Rugby World Cup. Ballymena had Jamie Smyth, Chris Henry and Bryan Young so there were good players on show.

UCD were relegated from Division 1 on the last day of the season due to that ridiculous last-minute 50-metre drop goal by the Young Munster scrum-half Mike Prendergast, who has just returned from coaching in France for ten years to become Munster's attack coach.

I was called into the Ireland Under-20s squad for training and warm-up games for the Six Nations before Christmas and was immediately struck by the quality of the backroom team. As well as Allen Clarke (head coach), we had Nigel Carolan (backs coach), Philip Orr (team manager), Philip Morrow (strength and conditioning), Emma Gallivan (strength and conditioning), Regina Flanagan (masseuse), Martin Joyce (bagman) and Vinny Hammond (video).

Carolan went on to be Ireland Under-20s head coach and assistant coach first with Connacht and then Glasgow. Morrow was brought over by Mark McCall to become a key part of Saracens' success and Hammond progressed to become video analyst with both Ireland and the British & Irish Lions. We had a really good squad too; Peter O'Mahony, Conor Murray, Nevin Spence, Jack McGrath, Rhys Ruddock, Dave Kearney, Dominic Ryan and Matt Healy, to name a few.

Training was normally in Ashbourne or the Johnstown Hotel in Enfield, Co Meath and I played at out-half in the Six Nations warm-up games against Leinster "A" and Ulster "A".

We won four out of five games in the Six Nations to finish second, beating France (9-6) and England (19-18) in our home games in Dubarry Park in Athlone, and also beating Italy in Piacenza by 29-23, before we lost to Scotland 35-20 in Perth and finished off with a 9-6 win away to Wales in Parc y Scarlets.

Personally, it was a mixed bag. I played '13' for the first four games before I was dropped for the last one in Llanelli when I played the last half-hour. I was the place kicker for the three middle games. There was a real scrap for that number

'10' jersey between Andrew Burke, Ian Madigan and myself. Andrew played the first game at out-half and was injured before returning for the last game. Mads played at '15' in those two and at out-half in the middle three games. The highlight of our campaign was undoubtedly beating England, when I scored 11 points from the tee as well as an assist for Michael Keating's try, but the last play of the game will live with me forever.

We were trailing by two points entering the last play of the game. We had to go through phase after phase to work ourselves into position until 'Mads' decided to take on a drop goal from at least 40 metres range and landed it. Dubarry Park went into raptures.

Losing to Scotland was not a highlight but I'm not sure I've ever played in a game which was dominated to such an extent by one forward. Richie Gray towered over the match, in the line-out and general play, and almost single-handedly won the game. Due to that defeat France beat us to the title on points difference.

The 2009 Junior World Championship, or Under-20 World Cup, was played in Japan that June. A 26-player panel was chosen in early May. We had to acclimatise to the eight-hour difference there in advance. This meant going to bed early, when it was still bright, so that our body clocks were in sync by the time we landed.

We had plenty of pre-World Cup training camps and went to Scotland for a warm-up game which we won by about 40 points, so we were in good shape. I sat beside Allen Clarke on the plane and we went through a preview of our opening game against Argentina on the 11-hour flight. I felt like a senior player at this stage because I was performing well, and I had just been given my first start with Leinster, so my confidence was high.

Our base for the first three pool games was in Nagoya and our results determined where we would be based for the play-off stages. My parents came out for the tournament as did three of my schoolmates, Alex Browne, Chris Fenelon and Andrew Lawler.

They booked the flights before I was picked, so once that happened, they were relieved. They told me: "See you over there" just before I left. They stayed in places that you could barely swing a cat in, and I only really saw them after games apart from one evening of karaoke. The Japanese love their karaoke.

Japan was brilliant to tour.

The people are amazing and must be the politest you could ever meet. I have particularly distinct memories of the massive skyscrapers in Nagoya. We stayed on the 78th floor. Every time we left the hotel on the team bus for training or a match, members of staff lined up outside to greet us and the same when we returned.

Meals in the team room consisted of a mix of Western European and local Japanese dishes. We had a guide with us the whole time and one evening we went on a full Japanese experience as a team.

We went to a restaurant where we were sitting on the floor, with a little barbecue at each table and we had to cook the raw food in front of us. Some guys tried the intestines but maybe regretted it the next day.

Another memory is of the changing rooms at the games being pitch side and entry onto the pitch was through sliding glazed doors. At games, locals had made signs for some players. For example, "Go Eamonn go" or "push hard" in reference to the scrum. Games were generally back-to-back, so the signs were switched when the next game happened.

We beat Argentina 16-9 in our opening match, Nevin Spence scoring a try, and I kicked 11 points. Against the Baby All Blacks, a misnomer if ever there was one, we decided to challenge the haka, which may or may not have been a good idea. The commentator that day, Nigel Starmer-Smith, was very unhappy with our actions and spent much of the rest of the match expressing his disquiet.

We defended heroically and restricted them to a 3-0 lead until past the 50-minute mark, before they scored two converted tries. In losing 17-0 we ran them closer than any team in the Under-20 World Cup the year before in Wales, when they beat Ireland 65-10 in the pool stages and England 38-3 in the final. They also went on to retain their crown in Japan, again beating England in the final by 44-28.

We then beat Uruguay 45-0, when most of us were rested. This meant we went to Fukuoka for the fifth to eighth place play-offs. Rhys Ruddock had to take the bullet train to Tokyo to sit his Welsh end-of-school exams.

However, we lost 19-17 to Wales, which put us in a seventh place play-off against Samoa. The day before that match, I passed by Allen Clarke in the hotel corridor and he pulled me aside.

"We'd like you to captain the side for this game. Would you like to do it?" There was never any hesitation in my mind. Our regular captain, Peter O'Mahony, was out injured but it was still such an honour, the biggest of my career to that point. The morale of the team was a bit low due to our result against Wales and our bodies were tired after 12 months of training without a break. I called a meeting before dinner and remember saying: "Unfortunately this will be the last time some of us will wear the green jersey, so leave everything you have on that pitch."

Little did I know that I would fall into this category.

It was a terrible match and we lost 9-3, meaning we finished eighth out of 16 teams. We had the squad to do much better.

After the Junior World Cup I had a few weeks off before returning for pre-season with Leinster and my second year (2009-10) in the academy. I had a few injury setbacks, straining and tearing ligaments in both ankles, which was frustrating, as this was the year to push on. Still, I managed to train and play regularly enough.

I was now starting games at '10' with the Leinster 'A's, including interpros and British & Irish Cup games. My second cap for the Leinster senior team was a repeat of the first, at Rodney Parade against the Dragons, on December 12th. I remember Cheika saying that this was the game to show how far we have come as a club as there were plenty of young guys making their debuts.

We stayed in the Celtic Manor Hotel, home to the 2010 Ryder Cup, as opposed to the nearby Holiday Inn the year before, so there were no excuses that the club weren't looking after us. We didn't return the favour and got a right bollicking after the 30-14 defeat. We let ourselves down that day a little.

Then came that fateful day on January 16th, 2010, when playing for UCD against Lansdowne, after which my rugby career, and my life, was never the same again.

FIVE

Italy Calling

THE DYNAMICS of my life changed when I received a phone call from my former academy manager Collie McEntee in early April 2013.

I was in Dundrum shopping centre with a bag in either hand when he rang.

He knew that I was keen to coach and the first thing he said was: "How would you like to move to Italy?"

I really didn't know how to react because this seemed so out of left field.

Collie had been speaking to Mick Kearney who has managed a few Irish underage rugby teams and I knew him well from his time as Irish Under-20s manager.

Mick had received a call from a guy called Ben Little who lived in Udine in the region of Friuli-Venezia Giulia, in North Eastern Italy, close to the Slovenian border. Like Mick, Ben is a Lansdowne RFC man and is the nephew of Mick "the kick" English who played for Ireland from 1958-63.

After my conversation with Collie, I rushed back to tell Cordelia and my family. To be honest, I was soon very keen on taking up the offer as I just wanted to get out of Ireland and follow my own path, but I spoke with Cords and my family about it. Cords was understandably apprehensive, but my family was ecstatic.

Initially, after my retirement, I had moved out of the family home in Whitechurch and into a house with my former teammates Ciaran and Rhys Ruddock, and Eamonn Sheridan, in Dundrum. I needed the independence, but it was also tough seeing the lads coming and going from training. I'd sometimes sit there not knowing what to do. When I had time on my own, that's when negative thoughts would creep in, so I explored different things I could do.

I re-sat my exams for the Sports Management programme in UCD. Thanks to Dr Olivia Hurley, I started a certificate for Sports Psychology in IADT-DL, Dun Laoghaire Institute of Art, Design and Technology. I went back to St Columba's to coach their Under-14s and helped a little with the seniors as well. I also helped with the UCD Under-20s and I became the head coach of the St Marys Under-20 Pennant team. Hugh Hogan, who since went on to become the Scarlets' defence coach, was the Under-20s first coach so we would see each other a fair amount.

Leinster were very accommodating in allowing me to watch training sessions, which I did a few times. They were mostly academy sessions but that was actually very hard for me. Too close to what had been my rugby home and my dreams.

On 9th February 2012, I actually returned to the site of my accident, the sports fields of UCD, not to play rugby, but rather to start another chapter in my playing career. It happened to be the same night Leinster played Treviso in the RDS, one year after my Man of the Match performance. However that same night, in the rain, I started a short-lived comeback to Gaelic football for Kilmacud Crokes in a match against the Dublin Minors. It was my first game in eight years in a Kilmacud Crokes jersey and I went on to play the rest of the season with the Intermediates. It was my attempt to keep playing high quality team sport, but in a different arena.

I trained with Jason Cowman, the Strength & Conditioning coach for Leinster at the time and now with Ireland, and a friend of mine, Chris Fenelon, for a half triathlon in aid of Christian Aid. The money raised bought sports equipment for a number of football teams in South Sudan, which Philip got to see first hand when he visited there in July 2012. This took place in the beautiful backdrop of Glendalough where we had to run up and down the Sugarloaf. Out of the three of us I categorically finished last.

I wanted to make the Leinster "A" schools more competitive so I went around all the different schools and met their coaches and teachers with a view to starting up a proper summer training programme instead of a couple of training sessions before games.

Andrew Adams, a teacher and rugby coach at Newpark Comprehensive school, helped me hugely and I worked with him at their training sessions. I wanted players to see that you could make it to the professional ranks even if you went to a smaller rugby playing school. I asked Ciaran Ruddock to help with the strength and conditioning side of things.

I coached at the Leinster summer camp called "The School of Excellence" which took place in Kings Hospital College. In previous years I had been there as a professional player giving advice to aspiring players.

After that camp, I met the rugby director at Kings Hospital who offered me a job to coach the seniors, both in training sessions and in covering a few lessons in the library. I declined this offer simply because it was all too similar to St Columba's and I had only left there three years previously. I wanted a completely different challenge.

So, after that call from Collie, I contacted Mick Kearney and he told me about the conversation he had with Ben. He subsequently forwarded a job description from Ben on April 19th, 2012. I read through the email and the job description seemed perfect: Technical Director of Leonorso Rugby Udine, overseeing teams from Under-6 to Under-20s.

Reading that email gave me life again.

I couldn't wait to go out there and see what it was like. Through Mick, we organised a time for Ben to call me and the next day, April 20th, he rang. We had a lengthy discussion about rugby and the position of the club.

He asked me: "Would you be interested in coming over here to coach?"

Immediately I said: "Yes, absolutely".

Any opportunity to get out of Ireland. I wasn't doing myself any favours either. On one occasion I went out on a continuous week of drinking. It's embarrassing to think of it, but I even went to a nightclub on my own. As it was a Sunday it wasn't even that busy, but I just wanted to keep on drinking and stay out rather than go home.

I woke up the next morning and thought: 'What are you doing?'

No harm done, but I was out of pocket and didn't feel any better, so what was the point?

One night, I went to the Dtwo nightclub on Harcourt Street. At one point I was out in the smoking area at the back of the club when a number of ex-St Mary's RFC teammates and Leinster Academy players saw me. They immediately came up to me and gave me a huge hug. It was the first time I'd seen them since I'd announced my retirement.

Right there, in the nightclub, I burst into tears. I hadn't even drunk that much but I needed to leave straight away by taxi with Cords. When we got back to Cords' house, I went up the stairs to bed and as I did, I punched two holes in the wall. This was all totally out of character for me.

There was no escape from who I was or my story. Not that I was a household name but whenever I went out to bars or nightclubs, guys my age would say to me: "Ah, it's a real pity. You were a great player. You had a great future".

It was the words 'were' and 'had' that got to me. These guys had all the best intentions but I'd had enough of Ireland. Rugby in Dublin is a complete bubble. I never fell out of love with the game but I needed a different challenge and a different country.

I'd always had a fascination with Italy and I wanted to help make their rugby a little bit better. Italian rugby is seen as the poor relation of the Six Nations and, if so, rugby in North Eastern Italy is poorer still. Udinese is a Serie A football team and rugby is a minority sport. But that was part of the appeal, and I wasn't going to be known. I could be anonymous.

I booked a flight for May 7th, 2012. I was flying on my own at 7am so was on an air coach at about 4am. I flew into Treviso airport where I was met by Ben Little and the Sporting Director, Gianmarco Stocco. Coming through departures you could already feel the humidity. They picked me up and drove me to a beach town called Lignano where the concept of beach rugby was created and, in fact, where the idea of hiring an Irishman to coach Leonorso was born over a few beers on the beach.

Ben and Gianmarco asked me what I liked to eat, and I said gnocchi, which is a potato dumpling dish served with anything really; ragu, cheese, vegetables. The portions were massive but I thought I should finish it, as much out of politeness if nothing else. That left me in plenty of pain and I was subsequently told that gnocchi expands in your tummy.

After a quick stroll on the beach, I was taken to the Astoria Hotel in the centre of Udine where many visiting Serie A football teams stay. It was about 4pm and I had a kip in the hotel as I had the next day to explore the town.

I was scheduled to meet Massimo Rizzi, a pretty successful businessman who had basically funded Leonorso and created my job, at 6pm so it was important to make a good impression.

His son Antonio Rizzi, the out-half who played for Benetton and now plays for Zebre, is one of the kids I coached at Leonorso and with his son being an up-and-coming out-half presumably Massimo thought: 'Here's a recently retired out-half who played for Leinster and the Ireland Under-20s to coach my boy'.

Later in the evening we went to a restaurant in the city centre called Ristorante Concordia. I met Massimo and his wife Daniela. Giorgio Leone (club president) and his wife Cinzia, Roberto Not (club photographer), Gianmarco (sporting director) and Giancarlo Stocco (rugby journalist) were also there.

I was still full from lunch but they continued to wine and dine me with an antipasto, primo, secondo, dolce, coffee and a digestif (usually a limoncello).

If you didn't like carbohydrates or meat you were struggling.

I had a very uncomfortable night's sleep, but I was excited about what the next day held.

The next morning, I went for a stroll around the city centre by myself and it really is a beautiful little place. That afternoon I went to see an Under-14s game which was to show me what group of players I would be dealing with the following season. The game was very one-sided with Antonio the star.

I must have put on about 3kg in the three days I was there. The Leonorso staff said normally they don't eat this much, but the club were trying to put their best foot forward and it worked. I loved the place. I returned to Ireland with not that much to think about.

I talked with Cordelia, but she was apprehensive. She is more attached to home than me, so it was more difficult for her. I think she felt a bit of pressure because she sensed I was going regardless, and that I needed this change. We weren't living together full-time so it would be a massive challenge not only taking that step but doing so in a place where English is not spoken too often. She had just finished studying a degree in Art History at UCD and worked in a wine shop, so I reasoned there would be no better place to go than Italy. Putting my interests before hers, she agreed to us making the move together.

On May 9th, 2012, I accepted the job via email.

Later that month, on the 27th, Cordelia and I flew out to Italy for the inauguration of the new facility at the Bearzi school where Leonorso trained. The club saw this as a good opportunity to unveil me as the new Technical Director and I saw it as an opportunity to show Cordelia around.

The training facility had a massive indoor area which was under construction, with a gym, offices and three pitches which had just been laid. It was situated in a secondary school run by the Catholic Church and the Bearzi football club were also neighbours. We were picked up by Massimo and Daniela from Venice airport in their white Volkswagen Golf R sports car. The journey would normally be about one hour and 20 minutes, but Massimo did it well under an hour.

We stayed in a different hotel in the city centre which was run by the parents of a player I would be coaching. I was really excited to show Cordelia around and we went straight to Piazza San Giacomo, one of the main squares, for a slice of pizza and a €1.50 Aperol Spritz.

The next day was the opening of the new club facilities. It was roasting hot, so choosing jeans was a bad decision. There were hundreds of kids from their rugby school programme and it was very well organised; giant inflatable welcome signs, multi-coloured t-shirts for all participants, a barbecue and music. I mostly kicked a ball with Antonio, teaching him how to spiral kick. This kid was talented.

During the next few days, we again had more food than was sensible. We were taken by Ben to a little remote town outside of Udine called Cividale, where the famous "Ponte del diavolo" (the devil's bridge) lay. This became one of Cordelia's favourite places and we were also shown the Stadio Friuli, where the Udinese football team played.

The night before we returned to Dublin, there was a meeting after dinner to finalise the details of my contract. I sat back and listened as all the club officials chatted away in Italian with Ben trying to translate for me. All seemed to be sorted.

As soon as we returned home, I started trying to learn the language through reading and apps. I looked up rugby phrases. I also began to plan how I would go about training sessions, sometimes forgetting that I would mainly be teaching 14/15-year-old kids.

Cords made a massive effort as well. She thought that she could teach English over there, so she attended an intense Celta course in Dublin City centre to qualify as an English teacher. She found it really hard, and it did put a fair amount of stress on her, but she passed and that was all down to her hard work.

I was really touched by Leinster when I left. The players, off their own bat, pulled together some money and gave it to me for a holiday voucher. To this day, I am incredibly grateful to them. Cordelia has an aunt and uncle who live on the Caribbean Island of Nevis where they have holiday houses on a beach. It seemed idyllic, and it was. We spent two wonderful weeks there, even managing to see a one-day international cricket match between the West Indies and New Zealand. It was perfect before starting our new life in Italy.

A couple of days before leaving, I had a lunch in Dublin with my nearest and dearest at the local Grange Golf Club. My whole family were there as well as my best friend Andy Lawler and his parents Peter and Louise, who looked after me as if I was one of their own throughout my teenage years.

The night before I left a few people called over wishing me good luck. There were a few tears from other people, but I was ready to go.

I moved over to Udine in August 2012 and Cordelia joined me a month later.

•••••

On August 23rd, 2012, I had set my alarm for 4.30am. Wearing the white and black jersey of Leonorso, which had been given to me by the club, I carried two big bags, one Leinster and one from my Irish Under-20s days.

I set off to Dublin airport to catch the 7.30am flight.

I touched down at Venice International airport and when I stepped out of the plane I instantly regretted not wearing something lighter. It was about 40 degrees. I was dropped to our new apartment where I started to unpack and prepare for a new chapter in my life. The apartment was in a quiet area, just outside the main city centre and there was an idyllic little archway which led into a small courtyard where you could park your car. I went for dinner that night with some of my fellow coaches.

After dinner, I was told that my new car was outside and I

would be driving it back to my apartment. My heart sank. I had never driven in Italy before, and it was night-time. I stepped out to see a lovely family sized purple Toyota Corolla Estate 1.6litre car covered with Leonorso Rugby Udine marketing.

Daniela told me to follow her but that made me more anxious as they drove quickly. I did lose them a couple of times, but I had a rough idea of where I was going until I got to roundabouts, which resulted in me driving on the wrong side of the road. But I made it. Luckily, I hadn't been drinking at all.

Being Irish, I think the assumption was that I drank a lot, but I really don't. In my playing career I had been so focused on performance that I never drank much and, to be honest, I couldn't hold that much either.

The other coaches there were all in and around my age, but I was still the youngest. One night soon after I arrived, they took me to the best bar in Udine called Taverna dell'Angelo, where I was introduced to a drink called Cuba Libre, which is rum and coke. One turned into several and I was brought back to my apartment. I woke up in a pool of sweat not only from the alcohol but the searing temperatures outside. I had no air conditioning, so I had to purchase a fan.

The heat in peak summertime, around 42 degrees most days, was stifling, unlike anything I had ever experienced. We had a pre-season training camp from August 30th to September 3rd in a place north of Udine called Tarvisio which is very close to the Austrian border. It was in the mountains and I thought if the temperatures were the same in Udine then there was no need for a jumper. How wrong I was!

It was freezing at night, so I had to borrow one of the coach's jumpers. The two other coaches helping me were Luca Mion, who spoke English, and Andrea "Gnappo" Costabile, who didn't speak any English. Nor did the team manager Bepi Tosoni, which was very funny at times but made organising things pretty difficult.

After one particular training session, we had pasta al pomodoro prepared by Bepi and a parent. He asked me if I wanted some grana (parmesan) over the pasta.

I said: "Scusa, non mi piace", meaning, "Sorry, I don't like it."

I might as well have told him that I was about to kill him. He was very insulted. This is when I realised how passionate Italians are about their food. I have since had a volte-face about grana and now I love it.

Cords arrived on September 15th. It was great having her with me, but we knew it was going to be tough. Things were made immediately tougher when I received a call from my friend Stew in the middle of her very first night in Udine.

I picked up the phone and he just said: "He's dead."

"Who's dead?"

"It's Nevin, Nevin Spence."

It didn't feel real, and Stew definitely had a few drinks on him, so I didn't believe him. I lay in bed again and Cords asked me what was wrong.

I told her: "Stew said Nevin is dead." I then went onto the BBC website and there it was – 'Nevin Spence killed in County Down slurry accident'.

Nevin had died along with his brother Graham and father Noel in the tragic accident on the family farm. I couldn't believe what I was reading. I had trained with him, played with and against him, and even roomed with him. This was shocking. He had all the ability and desire to play for Ulster and for Ireland for a long time. For his life to be cruelly taken away from him at the age of 22 made me realise how lucky I was.

Cords and I had to adapt to a completely different way of life and culture. We had to adjust to siestas and come to terms with everything being closed from 12.30 until 3.30, or even 4.30, because it was just so hot.

Not being able to speak the language at all made daily life really difficult. Simple things like going to the supermarket, any sort of shop or bar, were complicated.

After about three weeks of being in Udine, Cordelia and I signed up to an Italian language course at the University of Udine. We must have signed up to the wrong one as the level seemed way too high and there were loads of Spanish people so for them it was a lot easier. We were seeing other people picking up the language much quicker than we did. The best way to learn was putting ourselves in uncomfortable situations where we had to use it. Shops, the post office etc.

Cords would always carry around the Italian dictionary with

her. One day she went to the supermarket with her dictionary in her hand. She was looking for stock cubes and approached one of the shop assistants, asking: "Dov'è il bestiame?"

The girl in the supermarket, and a few others who overheard this, all laughed. It translated into: "Where is the livestock?"

These kinds of episodes knock your confidence. You just want to slink away and go home. Assistants at the counter would ask you simple things like, "Do you want a bag?" Or, "Do you have a loyalty card?" and you just stand there and say, "Non parlo italiano". They would just look at you.

What made life harder for Cordelia was the lack of work for her. She did a bit of English teaching but spent most of her time in the apartment which wasn't helpful. While I was forced to mix with people through my work and eventually picked up the language, it was much tougher for her to do so.

Also, we only had one car, a Toyota Corolla, and I needed it. Udine's transport system was OK. There were buses and there is a train station, but if Cordelia had worked outside the city it would have been tricky without a car.

Udine is a relatively small city. About 100,000 people live there. You'd see everything within a week or so. It's near the Dolomite mountains and the borders of Slovenia and Austria, so the cultural influences are more Germanic. Because of this you would think that more people would speak English but not at all.

It is a beautiful city in the middle of the Friuli-Venezia Giulia region, or, in short, just Friuli, between the Adriatic Sea and the Alps. The further north you go, the 'Friulianers' as they're known, are generally more reserved whereas the south is like an ad for Dolmio.

Once you get into the Friulianers' circle of trust and friendship you're there for life, but it can take a while. They can be a little cold to outsiders initially.

There are, of course, lovely restaurants but in those early months we hardly ever went out because I was coaching.

The club also employed me to coach and teach in about ten different schools, which varied in days and times depending on what kind of programmes they wanted to run. In Italy there isn't sport in school, unlike in Ireland where there are designated times for PE/sports. The majority of Italian schools have one PE slot each week. That could be just 45 minutes or an hour.

Some schools could finish at noon or 1pm, while more private schools would finish around 3 or 4pm. So, you could have kids who finish school early, then hang around bars or have a coffee or a cigarette, then maybe go home and do a little homework before training at 6pm.

Whenever I got messages saying: "I haven't finished my homework" it used to annoy me. I'd reply: "Well, you've had five hours to do it."

My day would begin at 8am when I went into schools to teach rugby as well as English, which would bring me up to around lunchtime. I'd start coaching again at around 4pm until 10pm or 10.30pm some nights because Leonorso had a senior team which started training at 8pm and we did two-hour sessions. That wouldn't have been my choice but that's what the head coach at the club did. So, my days were really long.

My only day 'off' was Saturday, and I would drive to watch an Under-6 tournament an hour and a half away. That didn't go down well with Cordelia.

On a Monday night there'd be an Under-14s training session until 8.30pm. I wasn't even the team's coach but because I was the Technical Director, I wanted to be present at everything. I coached mainly the Under-16s team, but I also started watching what the Under-20s and senior teams were up to.

Leonorso translates as Lion Bear, but that name no longer exists as the two clubs in Udine have merged and are called Udine Rugby Club. Leonorso also had good connections with Benetton Rugby so the Under-18s manager of the club, Massimo Breggion, took me down in his car to visit the then coach Franco Smith and the team in Treviso. I got down to the club, watched training, had chats with Franco and the 119 capped Italian international Alessandro Zanni who played for Leonorso when he was younger before we headed back to Udine.

In effect, I completely sacrificed personal time. My rationale was the more I worked the less I would think about what happened to me.

Everything was rugby orientated. Cordelia became annoyed with me because I didn't have a balance in my life. She found that really difficult. We were 22 and living together for the first time, and in a new country where we didn't speak the language.

Ben was great to Cords at the start by taking her up to vineyards and introducing her to people he knew. But I wasn't there for her, to make this move to a new life in Italy work for her. I was too fixated on making myself the best coach I could be as I could no longer be the best player in the world. I know it seems a bit warped now, but that was my outlook then.

In addition to the club, I worked in schools where I would take lessons for an hour at a time. I was meant to improve the kids' English and teach them rugby as well. I found the coaching challenging.

My very first training session was with two classes merged into one, about 50 teenagers aged 14 to 16 in a school gym. Fifty teenagers in your own language is challenging but I didn't have a word of Italian. Nothing.

I started speaking in English.

"Right, this is the pitch."

They thought I was saying "bitch".

Whenever I repeated this, they found it hilarious.

The kids picked up on every mistake I would make when attempting to speak Italian. Anything I would try in Italian would be met with laughter, but it didn't bother me because that was the only way I was going to learn.

When you can't communicate through sound it's amazing how many hand gestures you start using so we found a way. You had to learn the basic rugby words pretty quickly. But even so, I loved the coaching, and working in the schools was perfect for me as I was learning the basics, 123/ABC, and I also had to communicate with their teachers.

For such a sporting nation, I was taken aback that, at both primary and secondary school level, the kids were only allocated 45 minutes to an hour of sport a week and, in my case, for these kids in Udine, that was with me. One morning I went to the gym in Leonorso which overlooked the pitches and I saw a class of 12 and 13-year-olds running laps of the pitch for 45 minutes as their "teacher" sat on the halfway line looking at his iPad. How can a kid get inspired by that?

After eight months I began to understand a little Italian and have a few words but sentences still weren't flowing. After a year I began understanding most things and after 14 months I was speaking Italian. Then I did another course as I had a base to work with and that worked better.

Our ground floor apartment was small. Cordelia wasn't wild about it but I thought it was grand.

One of the neighbours would talk and talk to me for up to an hour in Italian. I wouldn't get a word in, or understand a word. When my dad visited and said "Ciao" that would be the green light for this neighbour to start speaking Italian. Then Dad could be stuck with him for half an hour. In hindsight it actually helped me, because the more he talked the more I learned.

When my boss's wife came to the apartment one day her ear

was also bent by him. She asked me: "Does this guy speak to you all the time?"

I said: "Yeah, what does he talk about?"

"Absolute rubbish. It makes no sense," she said. "So don't speak to him anymore."

We lived on the ground floor so we had no balcony, just a small area for a couple of chairs. We had one bedroom and a teeny, tiny kitchen, an en suite, and a little open area where you had a table, a couch and a TV, which the club provided. The building was so old and the walls so thick that the internet wasn't good. We had to keep turning the Vodafone key off and on. Sometimes I had to go to the club to acquire a stronger connection.

But we were a ten-minute walk from the city centre. We lived 100 metres from a famous Italian footballer called Antonio Di Natale, who had played with the Italian football team for ten years and was often the leading goalscorer in Serie A. His goals had helped Udinese into the Champions League the season I arrived.

I was presented with a personalised jersey, signed by Di Natale. It was promoted as the "two number 10s in Udine".

I think I saw him once, in his Maserati.

My Toyota Corolla was one of the longer versions, and was emblazoned with the club's name and logo. The Italians love branding, but the stickers would start to fall off after a few weeks. The concept of driving on the other side of the road was also a little tricky at the beginning! One day I drove down the wrong way and was blared out of it.

Mum and Dad visited about six or seven weeks after I moved to Udine. Cordelia's parents, Rosalind and Richard, and her grandparents, Patience and James, visited as well in October 2012, when the weather was still fantastic. Unfortunately, her grandad passed away soon after so that was his last holiday.

But whenever our respective parents or grandparents visited us I knew I wasn't on top form. While they wanted to be tourists and see things, I wanted to keep working and I felt that if I wasn't doing something, then I was becoming lazy. If I couldn't be a top-level player then I wanted to become a top-level coach. I was laying the foundations to fulfil that ambition.

●●●●●

After my playing career ended the way it did, my coping mechanism was simply to work most of the day, so I didn't have to think about what had happened to me. I was almost emulating my dad.

By doing this though, I knew that I was making things more difficult for Cords. I wanted her to explore Udine and the surrounding areas because I felt we may not get this opportunity again. But things were becoming progressively harder and lonelier.

I look back now and I certainly could have chosen better things to attend. That Under-6s tournament an hour away on a

Saturday morning was probably not the best thing to be doing on your day off.

The bickering between myself and Cords was becoming more frequent and became draining for both of us. It was an incredibly frustrating situation as we both knew that we weren't fully happy at that time. She was finding it hard living abroad and I was obviously still coping with how my life had changed. Trying to deal with those things alone is hard enough but to do it with all those other circumstances made it even harder.

We had long, emotional conversations and decided that it wasn't going to work in Udine for us as things were then. We were better off being apart for a while or else we would have broken up permanently.

She received a job offer in London to work with a wine PR company and she moved to London just before Christmas. There were things Cordelia wanted to do for herself in London.

We were definitely not breaking up but it was going to be a long distance relationship. We would try to see each other for a weekend every five or six weeks but the time always went by way too quickly. At times we didn't see each other for a couple of months but we were lucky that there was a direct flight between Trieste and London Stansted.

In London I would take the train and tube to where she was living which took almost as long as the flight. More often it was her flying over to me, and I could pick her up in the car.

She stayed in London for a year and nine months, and it

was hard being apart, but we were happy doing our own thing. Cordelia didn't have to deal with my moods and be alone in our home all the time, and I didn't have to deal with her being resentful and unhappy in Udine. She had friends and family in London and was enjoying her job.

Of course, when Cords went to London I ended up working even longer hours, and it was lonely coming back to an empty, cold apartment each evening.

But this was the life I had chosen.

SIX

Mi Sento Pesante (I Feel Heavy)

MY BROTHER Philip and his wife Julie travelled to Italy for a week at the beginning of April in 2013. They started their trip from Venice, stopping off in Verona, and for the last three days they came to visit me in Udine. If Collie McEntee's call a year previously had changed my life, their visit would transform it.

By the time Philip and Julie visited me for the first time, my sister Emma had been over while my brother Andrew came over later. I hadn't planned much for Philip and Julie's trip. Philip is an explorer and I knew he could find his own fun. Also, Julie was four-and-a-half months pregnant with their third child so that would restrict their movements but I knew they would be fine.

The weather was lovely. They stayed with me in the apartment. So I slept out on the pull-out couch. It was very crowded and made me realise Cordelia was right in wanting a two-bedroom apartment.

When they met me, they noticed that I was a bit moody, snappy and sarcastic. There were a few reasons for my grouchiness.

They suggested going to the beautiful port city of Trieste which was about a 40-minute drive from Udine and nearer the border of Slovenia. Trieste is a really fascinating city with a strong Irish connection. James Joyce wrote Ulysses while living in Trieste and there is a life-size statue of him, as well as a museum and cafés dedicated to him, because of the time he spent there. He fell in love with the city and viewed it as a home away from home, kind of like how I was feeling.

Trieste is a very important trading destination with its deep-water port being the gateway for Northern Italy. There are some historical sites such as Piazza Unità d'Italia, one of Europe's biggest squares, the Grand Canal and Miramare Castle, to name a few. The city almost seems to have fallen into place as it is protected by hills which are bursting full of vineyards, agriturismos and restaurants.

Because I was in a bad mood, I didn't even want to drive there so we walked to the nearby train station, although it's not the worst train journey in the world. In fact, it has to be one of the most beautiful coastal trips, along the Adriatic Sea, anywhere on the planet. Finally, at the end of the journey, you overlook the whole city of Trieste.

On the train, we chit-chatted a little but I was not myself. The sun was shining, I had my brother with me, who I had not seen in months, and we were going to have a nice day. But I wasn't thinking about any of that.

As I used to do then, I flicked through the rugby results on my phone. It probably wasn't good for me but I couldn't help myself. And there it was. The Heineken Challenge Cup quarter-final the night before. Wasps 28 Leinster 48.

Now Leinster had beaten teams before but when I looked at the team sheet, there was Devin Toner and John Cooney, who had played in that UCD game when I had my accident in 2010. Rhys Ruddock, my house buddy, Dave Kearney, Jack McGrath, had also played, and were all guys I had grown up playing with. In fact, I had played with the whole team. Nacewa, Boss, Strauss, Cullen, the list goes on.

Isa, Darce, Rob and Mike Ross scored tries against Wasps, while Ian Madigan had scored 28 points. And it just hit me instantly.

My first memory of Ian was in a car on the way to Lucan Sarsfields to play a Gaelic football match for Kilmacud Crokes. Gerry Greene, our coach, had picked us up and his son David as well as Ian and myself.

You could see from an early age Mads was really talented and very confident in his own ability. We were both born in

1989 and Mads is barely eight months older than me. The big difference was that he went to Blackrock College, which is the leading rugby school in Ireland, and I went to St Columba's. But it was also clear that all we wanted was to be professional rugby players.

With Crokes we experienced the joy of being teammates. He generally played in the forwards, while I was in the midfield or in the backs. But then that camaraderie maybe changed a little when we were competing for the same position with Leinster and in Irish Under-20 sides.

I was in my last year of school and he was a year ahead of me. He had played for the Under-20s the season before, in 2008, when Ireland had a disappointing World Cup, finishing ninth.

I had a really good season in 2008-09 in school and playing with Leinster Under-19s. Everything just went for me and I was brought into the Leinster academy ahead of him. I don't think Ian would have taken that very well.

We were teammates again for Ireland in both the 2009 Under-20 Six Nations, with him at out-half and me at outside centre, and the 2009 Under-20 World Cup in Japan, when I was at out-half and Mads at full-back. Andrew Burke, another 10 from Crescent College in Munster, also started a couple of games at 10 in the 2009 Six Nations.

Then this upstart from St Columba's, a year younger, was picked in the academy and Mads was in the sub-academy. So, apart from our Under-20s tournaments together, I didn't see much of him in my first year in the Leinster academy, 2008-09, as usually the full academy players trained with the first team.

For my first year and a half in the academy until my eye was injured, I think my game suited Michael Cheika's style of rugby whereas Ian's probably suited Joe Schmidt's. Ian had an electric pass, one of the best passes until this day, whereas I was a bit more physical and certainly liked a half gap. My kicking out of hand might have been a bit better but he worked his ass off on his place-kicking and even then his stats were phenomenal. His percentages were already in the '90s, which was crazy.

We have plenty of history. I do remember when I got my first cap against the Dragons in May 2009, in Rodney Parade, he made his debut off the bench in the same game when he replaced me inside the last ten minutes. It was a week before Leinster's first Heineken Cup final so Cheika rested most of his frontline squad for that trip to Newport.

I didn't drive at the time and when the squad landed back in Dublin Airport, Mads drove me home to my brother's in Churchtown. As I hopped out of his car he said, in a very sincere manner: "You played very well today."

Our families have a good connection too. His dad, Michael, would have chaperoned my Mum and Dad around Japan at the 2009 Under-20s World Cup. If he hadn't they'd probably still be in Japan! Larry Brassill, Ian's grandad, and my mum would often have watched our underage Gaelic matches together and they still stay in contact. There were plenty of happy memories and contacts between our two families, although they would have known we were fairly hot competitors at the time.

So, we were probably more rivals than friends, which was understandable. We were each trying to become the best in the same specialist position. In camp we wouldn't have hung out that much, although we have each other's numbers and there is a mutual respect there.

Our second game for Leinster was almost a replica of the first, me starting at out-half with Mads replacing me for the last quarter in another defeat by the Dragons at Rodney Parade.

But after my eye injury a month later, he leapfrogged me.

Ian even made the matchday squad for the 2011 Heineken Cup final when he replaced Johnny Sexton for the last couple of minutes. By April 2013 he had become a regular in the Leinster team and that night away to Wasps he scored 28 points in their 48-28 win.

I held nothing against him personally. Nothing at all. But knowing him so well probably made it worse. We'd travelled such a similar route and after reading those reports I couldn't help thinking: That could have been me.

It was also when Declan Kidney's time as Irish coach was coming to an end, and I knew Joe Schmidt was in line to take over. All I could think about was hearing more results like this, but on the international stage, for years to come.

Here they were having this glorious victory and I'm stuck on a train about to learn about James Joyce. What would I much rather be doing? Philip noticed that scouring my phone immediately had a negative effect on me, and that my mood worsened – more snappy, more sarky.

Both Philip and Julie asked me if I was okay. I was pretty casual and dismissive. I'd been having these mood swings for a while. But I admitted to them that Cordelia, now in London of course, knew that I'd been having bad mood swings for a while.

It was usually just one day a week and generally around result days, i.e. Saturday or Sunday, and seeing the names of my former teammates and friends playing with Leinster. I dealt with it by going to the gym and punching a bag, or just working it out of me. Given the fact that I'd moved to Italy in August 2012, this behaviour seemed to have gone on for the guts of an entire rugby season.

We got off the train to visit the many different sights and to tuck into the wonderful Italian cuisine on offer. But anything Philip suggested was met with a classic teenager's grunt or groan. I wasn't bothered to do anything. I actually just wanted to head back to my apartment.

If you go on holiday with Philip you'll be exhausted more than relaxed. He wants to do everything and see everything that's possible, on the premise he might never be there again, although with Julie being four-and-a-half months pregnant that limited his scope. After some lunch, we headed for the main area of San Vito where there is the waterfront, the remains of the old city and, of course, Piazza Unità d'Italia, which truly is beautiful. There's also the Teatro Romano di Trieste, Castello di San Giusto, which overlooks the city and everything to do with James Joyce. There was actually a film being shot there at the time so Philip was in his element.

We walked and walked, as my brother does, with a huge amount of enthusiasm and eagerness to learn about a new place and I felt sorry, not only for myself but also for my sister-in-law. Julie started to drift behind us a little bit, perhaps to give us some space.

Philip suggested walking up to Castello di San Giusto. When I saw the hill we would have to climb I tried to use Julie as an excuse to skip it, but up we went ahead of her. As it was just myself and Philip we had time to talk.

I can't remember exactly how I was triggered into breaking down but as we were going up this massive hill, I turned to my brother and he saw my eyes full to the brim with tears. I felt this huge pressure building inside of me and needing some sort of release. When I made eye contact with him, my defence walls came crashing down and I broke into tears.

All I remember saying to Philip was: "I can't go on. I can't go on!". Not by any stretch of the imagination did I mean I was contemplating suicide. Just that I couldn't continue being angry at the world, blaming other people and the weight of negativity which had completely overtaken me. And I didn't want to have my nearest and dearest stepping on eggshells around me.

At times I would think of Nevin Spence, my Under-20s

teammate, dying within four weeks of me moving to Italy. Nevin and I had roomed together a few times. We had very deep conversations about life and religion. He was a very religious man and was interested in what Horace did. And here I was moaning about my life.

As I cried and cried and cried with Philip, he responded in a way any good sibling would and simply put his arm around me. He knew this was a cry for help from his little brother. Philip signalled to Julie to hold back and we had a brief chat for about five or ten minutes but it was hard to get anything out of me amidst all the tears. The bottom line, I told him, was that I missed playing rugby.

I couldn't have predicted that outpouring, and I couldn't have predicted it being with Philip but, in hindsight, it made total sense. He is closest in age and we did share a bedroom for years so maybe for that reason I felt more connected to him at that time or, with Cordelia in London, maybe it was just seeing a family member. I felt like a little pressure had been lifted off me once I had that release of emotion.

We continued on our tour of Trieste until we hopped back onto the train, and Philip didn't bring it up again but he has had suicidal training and he knew an intervention was needed. They stayed with me for two more nights, came to a game with me on the Sunday, before I drove them to the airport on the Monday. But, Philip being Philip, he put his thinking cap on.

This was the beginning of my second opportunity.

• • • • •

Philip flew back to Ireland with a heavy heart after seeing me. He thought: 'I need to help my brother here? How do I go about doing this?' Philip is one of the most doggedly determined people you will ever meet. He will not accept no for an answer. He's like our dad. He works incessantly.

My brother has seen plenty in his young life. He went to Uganda and southern Sudan, both war-torn countries, when he was 20, which completely transformed his life. Instead of having a 21st birthday party, he had a concert fundraiser with all the funds going to African trusts and charities. He has seen poverty, he has seen death, he has seen all sorts. If someone is in need Philip will step in, all the more so if it's his younger brother.

He remembered watching one of my training sessions in Udine during which I played a crossbar challenge with some of the boys in an underage team, punting the ball from the 22 metre line. The kids were saying: 'Ian hit the crossbar.' So I hit the crossbar. 'That was lucky. Do it again Ian.' And I did it again. It made Philip realise that his brother had clearly regained some of his depth perception. It's just that he couldn't see out of his left eye, so how can we protect that eye? How do you start a project like this? Where do you begin?

Luckily, if Horace appears to know everyone, Philip knows even more people. It's ridiculous.

Philip conveyed how worried he was about me to a friend of his called Mervyn McCullagh. They had worked closely together on the Irish Council of Churches, where Mervyn was an Executive Officer. Mervyn is highly intelligent and helped Philip map out a potential plan of how to go about getting me back on the pitch through some concept of protecting the eyes of rugby players, as such things were not available then. He recommended people to contact.

Philip wrote an email to me on April 15th, 2013, exploring the option of playing again. In the first two lines Philip wrote: 'I've been reflecting a great deal since last week, about our conversation about your ambition to play again. I keep coming back though to two things; Risk and Limitation.'

These were the two things that needed to be addressed and Philip's solution was protective eyewear. If each player has eight studs on each boot (which amounts to 480 studs in total flying around the place for an 80-minute match), then players are going to get injured.

As well as that, in 2012 the International Olympic Committee had created history by permitting the now disgraced South African sprinter, Oscar Pistorius to become the first double-leg amputee participant in the Summer Olympics. This was thanks to innovative running blades developed in collaboration with the Icelandic orthopaedic prosthetics company, Össur.

Sport and technology clearly had a great deal to offer one another. Barriers were already being broken in other fields and what may have been unthinkable at one stage, was fast becoming achievable.

He wrote: 'On top of that you are down and desperately

frustrated at being unable to play. So, it's a lose/lose situation from whatever way you look at it. However, if you were to return, you would reverse all that. You would be an inspiration to tens of thousands of young people, you would be able to deliver on the skills and development invested in you and you would no longer feel the frustration you do. It would become a win/win. And yet it is to rugby you want to return. As you say, at the end of the day, it's the love of mud, scraped knees and sticking to diets that you miss the most. So, your desire and request are not selfish or egotistical, it is in fact good, heart-warming pure love for the sport, which any rugby fan or authority should respond most openly and positively towards.'

Philip began researching extensively. Nearly every day thereafter he sent me articles on goggle glasses, 3D work and rule changes within the International Rugby Board (now World Rugby).

Philip pointed me in the direction of UCD where I studied and played. At his behest, I wrote an email on April 29th, 2013, to David Fitzpatrick, a Professor in the department of Mechanical Engineering in UCD. David would later become the inaugural president for the new Technological University Dublin. I outlined my desire to get back playing and any help would be greatly appreciated.

On May 9th, David wrote back and apologised for the lateness in his response, but he had just started a venture between UCD and Beijing University which meant he was travelling back and forth. He also said he knew of me, and his aunt and uncle were parishioners in our church. Talk about a small world.

Philip had been talking to his friends about this venture and his colleague, Richard Carson, who also was a rugby referee, knew someone in the IRB. Richard contacted him to see if we could speak with someone about protective eyewear. Contact was made on 13th June via email with a research coordinator in the Technical Services Department called Marc Douglas.

I flew back to Dublin for four days specially to meet David Fitzpatrick in UCD and Marc Douglas at the IRB headquarters. Before starting our research, Philip and I thought we would have to travel the world for our answers, but they were on our doorstep.

I arranged to meet David in UCD on Saturday June 15th late in the afternoon. Philip came with me, and as it was the weekend the campus was very quiet. We walked into the engineering department, an uninspiring grey building from the 1970s. Then we went into a small office and met David.

The meeting was very productive and David was so accommodating. He suggested getting in contact with Enda O'Dowd who was the co-ordinator for the MSc medical device design at the National College of Art and Design (NCAD) in Dublin. David emailed Enda that evening (15th) to see if any design students would be interested in taking up the project.

Enda responded the following morning saying it could be tricky to find someone at this stage to take on the project. He thought it could be good for someone potentially next year but certainly not this year. But he would ask.

On June 17th, Philip and I met Marc Douglas of what was then the IRB in their then offices on St Stephen's Green. We wanted to know the IRB's position regarding the use of goggles in the sport. Marc had just started in his role. He indicated that the IRB were in the early stages of developing something, but didn't shed any light on what that was. We told Marc we were prepared to do plenty of the heavy lifting for him but he had a genuine interest in helping us.

On July 2nd, Enda emailed me to confirm that a student was willing to swap his-end-of year project for ours. His name is John Merrigan. He had eight weeks to complete the project so didn't have much time. But this was a huge break.

The next day we let Marc know via email that we had a student willing to design a pair of "rugby goggles".

On Friday July 5th, at 11am, Philip met Enda O'Dowd and John Merrigan at the Food Hall in NCAD. The IRB had briefed John about what they were looking for.

A month later, on August 6th, Philip had a meeting at the IRB head offices in Dublin with Steve Griffiths, who was their head of technical services, Marc Douglas, John Merrigan and Enda O'Dowd. In other words, all the key people in one room bar myself, but I Skyped into the meeting from Udine.

John presented his end-of-year project, his findings and three design concepts for the goggles. The best option was to have the goggles built into a scrum cap and this had me excited because it seemed attainable. The IRB representatives were impressed and taking notes. They suggested maybe sending John out to Italy to share his ideas with the manufacturing company they had been dealing with purely on the design aspects. I don't believe this trip happened and I do not know how much of John's ideas went into the final design. The University of Ulster and University of Bradford were also working with World Rugby on this but I never received any information about their contributions.

On October 31st we received confirmation that the IRB rugby committee had given their approval to proceed with the project and on November 20th a 'Global Law Trial' for goggles was approved by the IRB Council.

Philip organised a meeting with the sports optician Dr Donal O'Malley in Dixon Hempenstall Opticians and Eyewear in Suffolk Street in Dublin on December 30th. Dr O'Malley passed on the contact details for Dr Eli Peli, who is a Professor of Ophthalmology at Harvard Medical School.

Unconcerned by the festive season, Philip contacted Dr Peli on December 30th. Dr Peli was helping in the development of Google glasses and Philip was enquiring about cross vision and vision expansion. Dr Peli responded that day to confirm that they were working on a system to expand the field of vision in people who lost one eye. Dr Peli requested more information about the goggles and specific measurements of myself with, and without, the goggles. On New Year's Day, Philip wrote to John

Merrigan asking if he could share his project with Professor Peli in Harvard.

On January 6th, 2014, I called in to the IRB head office on St Stephen's Green to collect a prototype pair of goggles and headed to Dr O'Malley's shop nearby to get measured.

On January 9th, 2014, we had our first introduction via email with Francesco Rambaldi, the head of the design and manufacturing company in Bologna called Raleri. On the same day the IRB signed off on an agreement for the trial of rugby goggles to commence. Within four days registration for the goggles went viral. On January 21st I spoke for the first time with Francesco. I must have been on the phone with him for about an hour and a half. My spoken Italian was still not fantastic, but I didn't need to say anything.

I needed to register for a code to make sure the union I was buying them from had agreed to take part in the trial. There was a delay in the dispatch of the goggles. They were due to reach me on January 22nd but I finally received my first pair of rugby goggles when they arrived at my apartment in Udine on February 13th 2014 in a rectangular plastic casing. Inside the plastic box, there was Raleri advertising, an explanation about the IRB-led goggle trial, a thick black strap that had 'Raleri' written in white across the back of it and a goggle casing much like ones you would have for normal glasses.

I was so excited but at the same time I didn't really know how it would go. They came in a see-through plastic package, and I tried them on immediately. As I was trying them on in my sitting room, I struggled to understand how the Velcro strap worked but I eventually figured it out. I knew beforehand that a scrum cap would be needed for extra security, and to be honest that just looked a whole lot better.

There was thin grey padding on the inside across the rim of the goggles to make sure the actual goggle didn't come into contact with the skin or eye area. One pair of goggles cost €74 but I was given the first pair for free as it was a trial.

Initially they only came in one size. Now they come in two, one for an adult and one for a child. I put them on and walked around my apartment to get a feel for them. When trying them on it was like wearing a pair of ski goggles. They felt quite big as there had to be a distance from your eye area. If that part was too close, then it almost defeated the purpose of protecting my other functional eye.

They were made of polycarbonate which is a flexible yet rigid material. Strong enough to withstand a stud and flexible enough to use on a rugby pitch.

I was told to go onto YouTube and look at tests done on the material to demonstrate how good it is.

I found a video of an American shooting a shotgun at the polycarbonate material from about 15 metres distance and the material didn't break so, eh, that was comforting!

You could bend them slightly which was good as it was meant to fit around your face. When I tried them on first, they were quite clear to see through, but some dust had gathered on them from their journey, which started me thinking about how to clean them.

The original strap was quite big. I tried wearing the strap and goggles around my head, without a scrum cap at first, to ascertain what the most effective way of keeping them on. I walked around my apartment and shook my head around to simulate a tackle or running. After I tried them on the field, I found that having the strap around my ears was not secure. They would slip down a few times and it didn't help with my hearing so that would have made it extra hard to play. The solution was putting the strap up towards the crown of my head. It was more comfortable than putting the strap around the middle part of my head, which would become sore as the strap would be quite tight, but it had to be to stay on. Having the strap quite far up also meant that it stayed in place better when the scrum cap was put on.

As time went on, the strap got thinner, and you could choose which one you wanted. I preferred the thinner one as it was more comfortable.

On the day they arrived, I put the goggles in my training bag and went to coach like I did every day. I finished coaching with the underage teams and it was now time to try them out. It was a Wednesday night so there was no senior training but there was one guy from the team who was going to help me out. His name was Stefano "Milou" Milani and he played wing for the Leonorso senior team. He was a strong guy, so it was good to test them out on him. The rain was coming down and it was dark so not ideal conditions for a first impression. We were on this little back pitch, and we passed the ball. I caught some high balls and I hit the pad with him. The rain coming down and the low floodlights made it tough to see and that worried me, but I just ploughed on as I didn't want this to fail.

• • • • •

Once I finished my first 'training session' with the goggles, Luca Nunziata, one of the other coaches and a friend of mine, took a photo of me with the black, grey, and white jersey on with my goggles for the local paper. People laughed a little at me for the way I looked but that was to be expected.

Senior training was Tuesday, Thursday and Friday at 8pm and would sometimes finish at 10.30pm. For two nights of the week, we trained in a remote town called Tricesimo, which was about 15 minutes north of Udine, and then Friday evening was at the club. Winter nights could get down to -10 degrees so many layers were needed, and the impending addition of rugby goggles was probably going to make my face warmer.

The floodlights weren't great in Tricesimo so it made catching and passing hard which was good training for my depth perception. I was chomping at the bit to tackle people, but you would know which guys you could put a shot on in training or not. My judgement was incorrect one time when I picked out the biggest lad and went to tackle him as hard as I could. He fell like a sack of potatoes and let out a massive groan. It turns out he was from Calabria where rugby isn't massive, and he was only just starting to play. I felt terrible but all the other lads thought it was hilarious.

In between the lads laughing at the hit, my prime feeling was one of calm and of readiness as I got back into the swing and physicality of the game.

There had to be a point – an actual moment – when all the efforts, all the emails, all the late-night chats with my family and Cordelia, all the worries and the stresses, crystallised into me actually playing a game of rugby once again. I could feel the moment approaching. I knew I was ready. I knew I was close.

SEVEN

The Return

Sunday, March 2nd, 2014

FOR MOST people, that will be a day of little to no significance – just another day in the calendar – but to me it is one of the most important days of my life.

It was the day I made my return to the rugby pitch after an absence of 33 months and 11 days.

The senior Leonorso XV played in the Serie C Regional division (the lowest one) and we were due to play a team called Oderzo, who had beaten us in a previous round. There had been a massive fight during that game so there was a fair amount of bad blood.

Mum flew over a couple of days beforehand for the big day. She was there to support me like she did for all my games. On the Saturday, the day before, I went with Mum to a Leonorso Under-18s match and it was lovely having people coming up to us after the game wishing us the best the next day. You could really sense that people were excited for me.

That night Mum and myself just went to a local pizzeria for dinner, and I went to bed early. I had so many things going through my head whilst lying in bed, but I felt compelled to write to Philip. In an email, I basically thanked him for all this. If it wasn't for him, I wouldn't be having those nervous butterflies in my belly which I missed so much. Life had more of a purpose again!

I woke up and went to the club early for a mini rugby tournament in the morning, but I told Mum I would be back to pick her up for the game. This certainly wasn't my normal routine for a game in years gone by, but I had to work. I went back to my apartment and had lunch, packed my bag with the addition of a pair of goggles and drove to the home ground with Mum. The previous day and night, it had rained so much that Mum thought they were going to call off the game. Rugby pitches are usually not fantastically drained in Italy but thankfully our pitch had enough grass areas on it for the match to go ahead.

I arrived at our home ground again. The famous "terzo tempo" of Italian rugby – food and wine post game – was still going on from the mini rugby tournament so there were still plenty of people in the ground. Considering the gloomy weather, the atmosphere was brilliant. I went to the changing room, placed my bag there and went back out for a quick scan of the pitch.

As I was doing that, I saw the other players coming to the game. I knew what the level was like as I had been training with this team for the best part of six months but when you see opposition players coming to the ground with cigarettes in one hand and a McDonald's in the other, it is hard to stay focused.

The game kicked off at 3pm so I went out to kick at 2pm, which had always been my normal routine. I put on the black and white socks along with my newly bought pair of adidas Predators. I ran and passed a bit to get warmed up and did some place kicking. The pitch was indescribably bad, but I was striking the ball well in the warm-up.

I distinctly remember practising my place-kicking from various different spots and after landing several kicks from the halfway line and the touchline, I could hear a group of Oderzo fans stood behind me whispering, "Oh merda" between themselves, as if they knew it was going to be a long day.

We finished the warm-up as a team and headed back into the changing room for some last-minute instructions. I put on my headphones and listened to some pump-up music, a bit old school I know. Mentally I was ready for this game but there were still question marks as to how the goggles would work in a game.

When we emerged from the changing room, there were the kids from mini rugby cheering us on and each home player ran onto the field, hand in hand, with one of those players. There were a couple of Italian rugby traditions to go through before the game.

One, the ball would start in the hands of the home captain and be passed alternatively between both teams as we ran on. The second would happen on the halfway line where both teams lined up, akin to national anthems, and saluted the opposition by stamping your foot on the ground (a 'hip hip hooray' thing).

Pre-match routines observed, it was time for the kick-off. The whistle went and their out-half struggled to get a bounce for the kick-off because the pitch was so saturated. It was great to get a few early touches and test the goggles in a game-like environment.

But the second time I took the ball into contact the goggles slipped down my face and covered my chin. I quickly took my scrum cap off and put them back in the right place, making sure they were tighter. We won 65-5. As a debut, I couldn't have asked for more in terms of how I was feeling, both mentally and physically.

I also managed to score 28 points but ultimately it was just great to have my knees covered in mud again, my lungs burning, and feeling part of a team. When the game was over, we congratulated each other. I saw Mum and just gave her a big hug. With a camcorder in one hand, she hugged me with the other and we both started crying. Mum was struggling to talk and just said: "Oh Eenie." This was a throwback to my childhood nickname of 'Eenie Weenie' as I was the youngest and it was probably an indicator as well of just how anxious she'd been leading up to the game and during it. For me personally, I was just so happy to be back and for the game to have gone so well. I knew I could push my level of performance with these goggles but it would require time to get used to them.

What happens when they fog up? If it rains? If there's a long passage of play? Or they fall off? Amid all these thoughts, I wondered what areas could I focus on to make these goggles benefit me, and not hinder me?

But these considerations could wait until after a few beers in the changing room and then we would always head to a restaurant for a feed after the game. So I went with the team and Mum came along too.

I sent feedback about the goggles via World Rugby's player welfare page after every game. I would find out various things about them after every use. The most common things to fix were the fogging up and scratching on the goggle lenses.

I was given a pair of tinted goggles to trial which helped in sunlight. They were completely black to look at, but it was like wearing a pair of sunglasses while playing. I later found out that they didn't fall under the trial umbrella, so I was not permitted to wear them as they were deemed to give me an advantage over other players on a sunny day! Heaven forbid I'd have an advantage with my one eye!

We reached the play-offs to get into Serie B, but we lost our last game to miss out by one point. It was a blessing in disguise though as the club was losing a lot of the better players due to work, relocation, or retirement.

I played ten games in total for Leonorso and the level was equivalent to J3/J4 club rugby in Ireland. On our team we had a variety of people, from a Moldovan international prop, a butcher who mainly spoke Friulan (a language spoken solely in that region), a Sicilian student who didn't know the rules of rugby and a few Argentinians. At times it didn't feel like real rugby as I could go through a whole game without tackling one player or hitting one ruck. But it provided me with the opportunity to see if I still had the drive to go ahead with this. And I never hesitated about that for a moment.

In order to truly restart my rugby playing career I needed to do a few things. One was to be excused from the last year in my contract with Leonorso and two was to find myself an agent to secure a team to play with for the following year.

Massimo Rizzi, my boss, readily agreed to release me from my last year with Leonorso and helped me find an agent. I met a few feeder clubs for teams that played in the Eccellenza, which was the highest level of club rugby in Italy. I had offers from Serie A with the idea of me being a player/coach for one of their clubs, and I was pitched the alternative idea of training one or two days with the Eccellenza team and then playing for the Serie A team. I didn't like these proposals at all.

One day, I received a call from CUS Torino which was a Serie

A team based in Turin, 5.5 hours drive from Udine. They were looking for a player/coach for their first team. Again, it didn't really interest me, but their head coach was heading to a club in the Eccellenza, and I thought this could be my opportunity in case they were short of out-halves.

The coach was hosting a training session for those interested in playing for CUS Torino. The training was at about 6pm so I set off from Udine at 11am. I arrived at the ground in my club car where there were some of the current CUS team training in the gym. I met the coach, Regan Sue from New Zealand, and he explained to me and one other player what we were going to be doing. There would be three tests: on-field skill, fitness and a gym test.

I started on the pitch with passing and kicking. Regan said that my weak foot was better than the good foot of their current out-half. We then did a tackling grid where I was essentially tackling for two minutes straight.

I didn't have my goggles with me as I was assured that there was no contact, but they brought out one of their props to run against me and Regan said: "Now I know you normally use goggles when tackling so we don't have to do this." I didn't want the goggles to be an issue, so I just tackled away without them. I made all my tackles without the scrum cap and goggles.

The session lasted about 90 minutes in total, and I was wrecked. It felt like we did a whole pre-season in that time. The other player doing it was a young kid from San Dona, which is a town on the way back towards Udine. I was asked to drop him home, so we left quickly. We just stopped to get some fuel. I grabbed some snacks at the service station as I was starving. I didn't have a massive lunch on the way down either, but this was bad preparation on my part.

Once I dropped off the other player and I still had about another 90 minutes on the motorway back to Udine. I was shattered at this stage and the next thing I know I had weaved off the middle of the motorway and towards the guardrail. I clipped the right side of the car, spun around a couple of times back on the main part of the road and then hit the guardrail, this time head on.

It really felt like my life did flash before my eyes.

This all happened at about 130km. It was midnight so thankfully there wasn't too much traffic or else it could have been much worse.

I opened my eyes to my hands on the steering wheel, airbag out, expecting to feel some pain. I felt fine.

I got out of the car, and I was pretty lucky. The whole front left side had been smashed in which is the driver's side. People stopped to see if I was okay, and the police arrived. I called a few people, but the majority were asleep, but I eventually got through to Giorgio Leone, Leonorso's club president and he came and picked me up.

The car was a complete write-off. It wasn't my finest hour but luckily no one was hurt and a couple of days later I received a call to say that a team in the Eccellenza, the top tier in Italian club rugby, wanted to meet up and have a chat.

That team was Rugby Viadana and that trial led to me being signed by them for the 2014-15 season. The coach had seen enough. All for a modest €20k per year contract.

But the trip had paid off!

EIGHT

'Second Chance, Never Forget'

BARRIE McDERMOTT is an ex-rugby league player who had a very successful playing career as a prop with Leeds Rhinos, Great Britain and Ireland. What made him unique is that he played professionally and achieved all this with one eye.

As a child he lost his eye in an accident, but nobody knew until he retired. He wrote a book about his life called 'Made for Rugby' which I have since read and would recommend to anyone.

On March 20th, 2014, Philip contacted him and the next day I emailed him looking for some advice. He responded within 20 minutes and suggested meeting up at a Rhinos game in the future.

I booked a flight to Leeds on the morning of July 17th. Leeds were playing Castleford at Headingley that evening. I arrived at the ground at 1pm where I met Barrie at the gate house entrance. It was a warm sunny day and Barrie gave me the warmest of welcomes as I thanked him for meeting me. He showed me around the ground and we had a good chat about life and our rugby experience through different codes. He asked me about my situation and described some of his career and life. I'd say we sat in the grandstand chatting for about two hours. I wanted his take on what it was like to play with one eye.

Barrie is a tough guy and was generally seen as an enforcer, so I don't think he ever gave it much thought. I asked him for what advice he had for me, given that he had gone on to enjoy such a fantastic career, and as we sat in the stand at the ground, he said: "We are who we are, forget the level you were at, be excited about the level you're at now and where you go from here."

It was advice that stayed with me throughout my career and also made me realise that to reach my new level, like him, I needed to do double the work at everything compared with everyone else. His words really motivated and helped me. They were words from someone who had won leagues and championships.

After our chat the crowd began gathering and Barrie was clearly at the heartbeat of the club. Everyone knew him and he knew everyone. He was signing autographs and posing for pictures as we made our way to the back of one of the stands where all the TV trucks were parked. Barrie worked as a pundit for Sky Sports and he introduced me to one of his friends who worked with him as a presenter. It happened to be Brian Carney, who played for Ireland both in league and union and had a spell at Munster. We chatted a bit and he was interested in what I was trying to achieve with the goggles.

Barrie gave me a ticket for the game, so I watched it and then headed to stay the night with a mate of mine, Adam, who was over visiting his family. Adam happened to be the guy in the hospital room when I was told by the doctors that my sight couldn't be recovered.

Barrie and I have sent each other messages over the years and he remained massively supportive of my attempts to play the game at the highest level again, starting with my time at Viadana.

• • • • •

Once Viadana showed an interest, I drove down from Udine to meet my agent near his town, San Dona, which is on the way, and from there to Viadana would have been a couple of hours. We met the powers that be at the training complex of the former Aironi club, which competed in the Pro12, called the Lavadera Village. We sat under the sun discussing terms and conditions over some lunch.

Three years previously, Leinster had played against Aironi and I was the "23rd" man, so I essentially ran water and provided messages to the players from the coaches.

'SECOND CHANCE, NEVER FORGET'

The Viadana Director of Rugby said: "I remember you in that game and you played really well". He must have been confusing me with another Ian who played that day, but I wasn't going to correct him if it helped my chances.

Because I had the goggles, they did have some reservations and offered me a one-year deal but with a review to take place in September, three months into my time there. If they weren't convinced, then they could let me go. The deal was signed. I was heading back to professional rugby.

I needed to find a place to live as Viadana was not exactly a hive of social activity and with Cordelia coming back over from London we needed a bigger city for her to find a job. We decided on Parma, which was about 30-40 minutes away from Viadana depending on traffic. The home of Parma ham and Parmigiano nestled in the region of Emilia-Romagna.

Trying to find an apartment in Parma when your Italian is not 100 percent was tricky but after I had viewed a few places, Viadana contacted me to say they had an apartment for us through a contact there.

This was a huge relief as I didn't want to be dealing with estate agents, especially when I didn't understand half of what they were saying. However, less than a week before moving in, the apartment we were promised wasn't available anymore.

I had to find an alternative apartment quickly. Luckily, one of the places I viewed was still available. When I called the estate agent describing the necessity of getting this place, she called the landlord immediately and explained my situation. The landlord was from Sicily and needed to be present to sign the relative documents. He casually drove 14 hours to meet us at the apartment.

While he was doing that, I was sent a whole load of documents in Italian which I had to sign on the day of the meeting, none of which I understood but I just went with it. I didn't really have anything with me that the estate agent had requested but thank God the landlord was from Sicily because he was so laid back. He implied all would be fine, and it was. I actually felt very proud that I was able to secure somewhere to live in a different language. He took me out to dinner even though I wasn't meant to be staying there that night. All lost in translation, but it worked out.

I had trained so much on my own prior to Viadana's pre-season that I knew I was in good shape. I didn't want to have question marks over me, and especially the goggles, in my first step back into proper rugby. This was all confirmed when I scored the highest in fitness and strength test scores. I normally wasn't at the top of these tests. Whether this was a case of me being in really good shape or the others not, I didn't know. Either way, I had hit the ground running.

Day three of pre-season started with some contact drills, so on came the goggles. My teammates just looked at me as if to say: "What is going on here?" But they quickly became used to this. A few asked me after training why I had to wear them.

'SECOND CHANCE, NEVER FORGET'

Our head coach made training physically very demanding and with the searing summer temperatures it certainly made my head extremely warm with all I had on. The group was a good mix of ex-Italian internationals, 7s players and young, up-and-coming players, and I was just so excited to be part of it. I went to and from training with a smile on my face because it just confirmed how much I loved the game and also I knew my performance at this level was going to be good. It gave me a huge amount of confidence and motivated me more.

As well as the way I was feeling about my efforts on the training pitch, I also felt like I had to fulfil my promise to myself, and something I wrote on my wristband before every game: 'Second Chance, Never Forget.'

At Rugby Viadana there was also another phrase that suited my rugby rebirth perfectly: 'Mai Mular' which meant 'Never Give Up'. I didn't want to have any regrets about my 'second' career. I wanted to push the boundaries, to show people what could be achieved, despite what had happened to me. My story, my career, was different.

I was made vice-captain for the season. In Italy before kick-off the referees would be given a folder of information and documentation about the players in any given game and I had to keep a doctor's letter (in Italian) and a copy of the World Rugby Goggle Trials page, ready for potential inspection or queries by a referee.

I wasn't the only one in Italy making strides with the goggles.

Prior to signing for Viadana, I was made aware of a former Perpignan and France Under-20s player who completely lost the sight in his right eye a few months earlier. His name was Florian Cazenave. He was not allowed to play in France because of their rules regarding sight loss, so I contacted him and told him about the rugby goggles.

It so happened that we had played against each other in the Under-20s Six Nations back in 2009. He moved to Italy, to a city very close to Parma, and played for a club there, and we actually played a pre-season friendly against each other. It was a very surreal moment coming up against someone in the same position. We ran out first, as we were the away team and, as I saw him, I just went up and gave him a handshake and a half hug. I don't know if he appreciated it or not, but I had admiration for him because I knew it wasn't easy and he was starting off on his journey with them.

We played our home games in the old Aironi stadium which had three nice stands and could have a capacity of around 10,000. The sound system around the ground worked pretty well and every time we scored points the song "Black and Yellow" by Wiz Khalifa would boom out.

This song was picked by the players as our jerseys were black and yellow but the announcers in Italy would always find Ian really hard to pronounce. So, I'd generally hear: "Meta (try) da Yann McKinley." But it felt so good though being in that environment again.

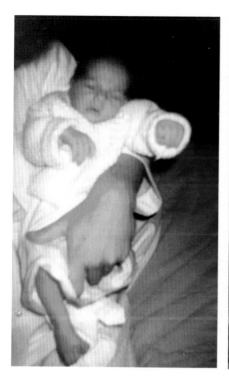

I was born in the Rotunda Hospital in Dublin on December 4, 1989, weighing 7lbs 6oz. Here I'm being held in my mother's arms and, apparently, I was the worst sleeper out of all the children!

Here I am relaxing on holiday in Roundstone, Connemara in September 1992. In the background you can just about see the beautiful – and wild – Atlantic Ocean

In this old family photo, my brothers Andrew (in red) and Philip (in green) teach me the fine art of scrummaging. Dad was a hooker so it ran in the family...

Trying on my St Columba's uniform in 2002. It was always a case of buying a blazer too big so that you could get a few years' use out of it!

Here I am in 2003 with my Kilmacud Crokes teammates, winning for the first time in the club's history, the Under-14 All-Ireland Féile in Galway

Me leading out St Columba's (below) against Gonzaga College in the Vinnie Murray Cup in March 2008. The pitch was a fair walk from the dressing room so I used the time to give the lads a bit of a pick-me-up talk

In action at the 2009 Under-20 Junior World Championship in Japan for Ireland against New Zealand

Scoring a try in 2011 for Leinster in the Magners League at the RDS against my future team, Benetton Treviso

One of the most important days of my life (above). 33 months and 11 days since my last match, I was back on a rugby field playing for Leonorso v Oderzo in Udine on March 2, 2014. When the final whistle blew, I walked off and embraced Mum

I'm pictured here with Florian Cazenave after a match against Rugby Reggio in September 2014. He had also lost the sight in his eye playing and started using goggles so he could continue. We had previously played against each other in the 2009 Ireland v France Under-20s Six Nations match

These goggles allowed me to return to the field of play and return to the sport I loved. We experimented with an additional prism to help me expand my peripheral vision. I visited Dr Eli Peli at Harvard University in a bid to design the best possible goggles and help me see defenders tackling me from the left side. The prism was not able to be used in matches

My time at Zebre was an enormous challenge and privilege and the Connacht v Zebre match in the PRO12 in October 2015 was a huge catalyst for the #LetIanPlay campaign. The IRFU refused to allow my goggles to be worn for this match so I could not play. That prompted massive support from both sets of players. Indeed, this picture has never been published before because some of my Ireland Under-20 teammates were essentially supporting a cause against their own employers' wishes

A 2016 European Rugby Challenge Cup game v Gloucester at the Kingsholm Stadium. I took a knock to the chin which required a fair amount of stitches

A momentous day. Winning my first cap for my adopted nation against Fiji in November 2017 and (below) kicking my first international points during our 19–10 win. Our defence coach Marius Goosen is behind me holding my scrum cap and goggles as I go to kick – I always kicked penalties or conversions without the goggles on

My family almost missed my international debut as there was a pilot no-show for one of their connecting flights. Luckily, they got there the night before! The security at the game was tight and trying to get this photo on the pitch was very difficult. A reluctant steward ended up taking the picture

Here I am with ex-teammate John Cooney swapping our jerseys after the Ireland v Italy game in Chicago in 2018. We would have played a lot as a half-back pairing growing up in Ireland

Running to see my family after my first game in the RDS for five years. I struggled to keep the tears away as I approach my brother Andrew

In a footrace against Jonny May and Elliot Daly of England at Twickenham and (below) meeting Irish president Michael D. Higgins before the RWC 2019 warm-up match against Ireland in August 2019. This would be my last international appearance

Captaining Benetton Treviso v Ulster at the Kingspan Stadium in Belfast in the Pro14 accompanied by my niece Izzy and nephew Cameron. Cameron is now much taller than me, so it was a good thing it was done then as he would dwarf me now!

Passing the ball to Italian teammate Federico Ruzza (below) while John Cooney and Devin Toner, who both played on the day I got injured back in 2010, look on

Becoming the first goggle-wearing player to represent the famous Barbarians Rugby Club

Clearing for touch for Benetton Treviso against Harlequins in the pouring rain at Twickenham Stoop

Cordelia and I enjoying ourselves in the Prosecco area of Valdobbiadene. It was only a 45 minutes drive from Treviso, so it was lovely to chill out up there from time to time and (right) with our son Malachy, who was born in December 2020

'SECOND CHANCE, NEVER FORGET'

The pre-season went well, both for me and the team, so the 'review' of my performances with the goggles, which was due in September, was quashed. This proved that I was heading in the right direction. My agent was even telling me that bigger clubs were inquiring about me.

The goggles made their European debut in a qualifying competition which the tournament organisers had introduced in 2014-15 for the Challenge Cup, when Viadana played El Salvador of Spain. We won 36-7, the sun was shining, the goggles were absolutely fine and it was an important step for the goggles to finally be worn during a European tie, even one taking place at quite a low-key level.

One of the most memorable moments at Viadana in that first season occurred when our club captain Roberto walked over to me one day with a question. "Ian," he said. "Would you be offended if everyone did a warm-up in the captain's run with one of their eyes covered? The lads want to know exactly what it is like to play like you do." It was an interesting request and I willingly accepted the idea as I thought it would be intriguing to see how everyone got on. Needless to say there were a lot of dropped balls and more than one of the lads came over and said: "Ian, I don't know how you do it."

Our season ended disappointingly as we just missed out on the play-offs on the last day, but I played every minute of Viadana's 18 matches, scoring 143 points, and I was voted second-best player of the championship by the general public.

SECOND SIGHT

In the middle of the 2014-15 season, I was invited to play for the famous Barbarians in a game against Heriot's in Edinburgh to mark the 125th anniversary of both clubs. It would be the first time the goggles were to be worn in the famous black and white jersey and also the first time in Scotland.

The Barbarians team had Scottish internationals Scott MacLeod and Gordon Ross in the squad as well as British and Irish Lions Ali Price and Josh Adams. Everything I heard about a Baabaas camp was true; plenty of laughs and a little bit of drinking in between training sessions. We even had a mini fitness session the morning of the game to get rid of the cobwebs from the night before and the beers clearly had little effect on our performance as we ended up winning the game 97-31 – surely a good advert for a night out with your teammates...

Meanwhile, Dr Peli and I had remained in regular contact. I sent two pairs of goggles to him in Boston for him to study and see if a prism was workable, but as this was a non-funded project it could take a long time. He suggested a face-to-face meeting might be the best step to take next, so I booked a flight to the United States.

On January 9th, 2015, Cordelia and I travelled to America for a two-week holiday, and for me to explore a prism that could be used to expand my range of vision.

First we went to New York for five days where we saw all the sights. I played with an American international at Viadana called Nick Civetta who was from there, so we were going to hang out with him and his family as well. We became very good friends from our time playing together.

We then went to Boston for ten days. We should have spent more time in New York but in Boston our first stop was Harvard University. The campus was like something out of a Hollywood film and Cordelia was just in awe of its beauty. I almost felt myself becoming more intelligent merely by being on the grounds!

Dr Peli had an office to himself, whereas the other professors had a communal area. We knew beforehand that this man was highly intelligent, and this was reinforced when we saw all his awards and articles about him on his office wall. We talked for a while about my story and what he did. He explained that he would be observing the findings of this study but that his understudy, Jae-Hyun Jung, would be doing the hands-on work with the prism concept.

Jae-Hyun first brought me into an observation room, akin to a normal optician, where he checked what my sight was like and what degree of vision had been lost due to my detached retina. I also did a test with the goggles on and it was interesting to find out that as much as 10 degrees of my vision, on my left side, had been compromised due to the goggles, and in particular the padding on the inside which meant I saw less.

As I sat in the chair, I was presented with what looked like a broken piece of glass, but it was the prism. It was maybe the size of a tangerine segment and some parts of it were ridged. The prism had to be screwed into my glasses as it would be placed on the upper left part of my right lens. Essentially, I would be looking straight at the prism, and it would reflect the images on the right side of my eye to enable me to see more on my bad side.

They asked if I minded having a hole screwed through the frame of my glasses so the prism could stay in place. I had wooden frames at the time, so it was easy enough to do. The prism had to be shaved into a shape that would suit my requirements, for example accommodating the contours of my nose, so there was plenty of placing, questioning and replacing.

"Can you see better or worse with it here?"

Eventually, after a few hours of this, I could look to my left and see almost to the same degree as I could prior to my injury. It was a surreal moment and I kept putting my hand to the side where I couldn't see previously but this time I could. The only drawback was that it created some double vision. I walked around the room and the corridor to get a feel for this new creation and I was advised to go and walk around in public.

I went for a stroll with Cordelia, and then into a supermarket. Several customers held their glance when they looked at me as there was, quite clearly, a shard of glass on my glasses.

Normally, in crowded areas, I would have Cordelia on my left-hand side so that I wouldn't bump into people. I didn't need her as I could see if someone was just about to pass me, but the double vision was difficult to manage. We returned to Dr Peli's office and I gave him some feedback about what it was like. They asked me: "Would you mind wearing these cosmetically?"

I said: "No, just as long as they help me."

It would be a huge help for driving as I wouldn't have to turn my head so much to see if there was a car parallel to me and I could see better if a car was passing me by. But I really wanted to know what rugby would be like with the goggles. Again, there was a process to be followed with the goggles as they were a different shape from my glasses. Once this was done, I could walk around with them like I did with my glasses, but until I trained with them I couldn't get a full sense of what it would be like.

This happened all in one day, but I was told to come back the next day, or day after, to make some final adjustments as the team wanted to be sure of their measurements. The next day Cordelia and I went back, but this time only for a couple of hours. I thanked Dr Peli and his team for all their time and effort.

He said: "Your brother must love you very much".

I was to take the prisms in my glasses and goggles back to Italy where I would trial them in more real life and training scenarios, and then give them more feedback.

This was going to be a new challenge, getting used to this prism. I drove my car around with it in my glasses and I found that so beneficial, even more so in Ireland because I would have the whole car on my left-hand side.

The negative side of the prism was that it was made of glass so legally I knew they wouldn't be permitted in rugby. Also, if it was to shatter there would be pieces of glass floating around the inside of your goggles, which wouldn't be the smartest thing. So, I didn't do contact work in training with them, only skills.

It was hard to adapt to them and the double vision worsened. My hand-eye coordination also seemed to revert to when I had my accident, and I didn't want to compromise that because I needed my right eye working hard and well for me to continue playing. The prism for playing and driving was ditched but it gave me hope that there might be something else down the track which would help.

The goggles I would have used for games then became my goggles for training. I would check my bag the night before training to make sure I had a pair in there and that they were clean. I always checked the weather forecast and if it was going to be bad I would bring a couple of pairs with me. I'd also bring a better pair with me when we were doing a contact session, but sometimes I trained without the scrum cap if I knew we were just doing skills or kicking.

I did a huge amount of hand coordination exercises both at home and at training, and both with and without the goggles. I used reaction balls and tennis balls to help with my coordination. I was shown a different way of trying to catch a ball which I practised pretty much every day. Normally a player would just put his hands out and catch the ball, but I was told to try keeping my hands in line with my vision and put them to the ball. This was easier when the ball was coming from a setpiece, i.e. a scrum or lineout, but not in general play as I didn't have time.

I'm left-footed and blind in my left eye. My favourite and most effective kick was the spiral but when I dropped the ball onto my foot sometimes I couldn't see it, which affected my accuracy. I had to adapt my body position by opening my body up more and kicking more laterally. I probably tried to force this too much and should have stuck with my instincts instead of trying to look for a perfect solution. A bit of a regret.

In the early stages of using the goggles, I also did a fair amount of tackle technique, and I tried to defend differently with my inside defender. I would have to trust my teammate more. You are always taught to come up square, but I found this hard. I worked on coming up at a slightly different angle so I could see my inside defender. I found defending toward the right wing difficult, which usually happened after a few phases, as you were a bit more exposed, and if I didn't see my inside defender then I would struggle to make a decision.

When I first resumed playing in 2014, I'd just use one pair of goggles but I quickly realised that I would need more, especially if I was going to be playing at a higher level.

I was sent some pairs for free and I bought more at a discounted price of €50. I figured out that I needed five pairs of goggles with me for matchdays. These needed to be clean, unscratched and without little smudges that sometimes appeared between the lenses.

If I was starting, I'd have one for the warm-up, one for the first half and one for the second half. The two physios circling the pitch would have one each just in case something went wrong. If I was a sub, I still did the same, although that might mean having one extra pair of goggles to use by the time I went on.

Those physios would also carry a towel, like for a hooker throwing the ball in, to wipe my goggles if the weather was particularly poor to help me see. Floodlights at some grounds were tricky so high balls sometimes were more difficult to catch but I just put my hand up to cover the glare and caught the ball. I think my GAA background helped me considerably as I was solid under the high ball regardless of the goggles. But it was definitely easier to catch high balls in daytime.

The goggles could become quite dirty very quickly depending on the weather, which meant playing with them in Italy was beneficial as it rarely rained. I used a standard glasses cloth along with a glasses spray to clean them regularly after I looked at different cleaning methods such as pull away strips that Formula 1 racers would use, as well as all the different types of cleaning products and anti-fog measures.

Invariably though, conditions for some games were worse than others. Playing for Viadana against Rovigo in the Eccellenza was my first experience of a game in wet and muddy conditions at a professional level. The goggles and the scrum cap were ripped off my head as I was driving for the line. I just continued until the referee blew his whistle, which was about ten seconds later. It made me realise how much more I needed to work and adapt my game in those conditions.

That was not the only occasion when playing in bad weather conditions made playing difficult.

After I won my first two caps for Italy in November 2017 – more on that later – I was on the bench again for our third game of that autumn series against South Africa in Padova, when the rain was torrential.

Soon after the 50-minute mark Marius Goosen, our defence coach, put his hand up to his earpiece to hear what was being said to him, presumably from Conor O'Shea, the head coach.

Marius then asked me: "Are you okay to go on?"

"Yes," I said.

I wasn't going to say no but of course when you can't see clearly, it makes playing against players like Handrè Pollard and Eben Etzebeth that much more difficult. I never wanted coaches not to pick me because of the goggles and I never wanted to make that an excuse.

In another Challenge Cup match against Harlequins in December 2019 the torrential rain made it predominantly a forward battle, which was fine by me, but my basic skills were put under huge pressure.

If I opted for extra padding on the goggles it reduced my

vision by another ten degrees. It wasn't just rainy days either, the glare from the sun could also affect my vision.

Due to the visual impairment – and the need to check the weather forecast endlessly throughout the week – playing with the goggles was a constant challenge but one I was also happy to accept and embrace.

After all, just getting to this point had been a huge battle in itself and one that had tested me every bit as much as my subsequent efforts on the field.

NINE

The Campaigns

BY 2015, 23 nations had signed up to World Rugby's goggles trial, including some of the biggest rugby nations; New Zealand, Wales, Australia, Scotland, South Africa and Argentina. Only three leading rugby nations hadn't signed up: England, France and Ireland. So, any player who used the goggles was not permitted to play with them in those three countries. These rules only pertained to contact rugby, non-contact rugby was always exempt from this.

We therefore had two options; one was to encourage the remaining three nations to sign up to the trial or the other was to encourage World Rugby to conclude the trial and turn it into law for all countries. We also explored the trial being split into two parts, one for underage and the other for adults, as the issues were different for both groups.

In the end, we felt the strongest case was to encourage each

Union to sign up to the trial. However, each of the issues relating to the goggles in the three countries differed, each affected my career in different ways, and each required different campaign approaches to get each rugby authority to sign up to the trial.

For example, England and France's opposition affected my ability to play European club rugby, which would have meant one or two important away fixtures each year. However, Ireland's opposition was the most serious, as it was the only country out of four in the then Pro12, which would not allow me to play in any away fixtures in that competition.

Ireland's opposition was made worse by the fact that I was an Irishman, who was a product of Ireland's development programme, who had acquired a freak rugby injury in Ireland and had worked hard on a creative safety solution to return to rugby, but now felt that I was being blocked in the process.

• • • • •

Ireland campaign 2015 (IRFU)

While Ireland's opposition affected my ability to play in a cross-border European competition, in many ways it affected underage Irish-based players even more than me, because for them it meant the difference between playing or not playing at all.

When the goggles trial began, it exposed that a whole

number of discrepancies existed, with many underage rugby players using a range of unauthorised forms of eyewear from other sports. It seems the IRFU's rules and local practice didn't quite align. One popular brand for example were Rec Specs, which a number of opticians fitted and supplied for underage players.

The trial therefore brought this issue to a head, as there was now one permitted, approved prototype in the world, which meant that all other goggles were now clearly invalid (as in fact they had always been anyway). In the case of Ireland, who were not part of the trial, this led to a clamping down of all forms of protective eyewear, but without any alternative option for players to utilise.

As a result, a number of Irish underage players suddenly began to be blocked or prevented from playing rugby by club officials or match referees. Therefore alongside their parents, these players started to launch their own campaigns.

For example, in August 2015, seven-year-old Ryan Totten from Coleraine in Co Derry/Londonderry was told that he couldn't play rugby anymore. As a consequence, Ryan's mother Christine launched a campaign which was supported by the former Irish captain Willie Anderson.

In October, the same situation arose and a father launched a petition to lobby the IRFU on behalf of his son. In November, a referee prevented two players for Portarlington Under-13's in County Laois from playing at the start of a match, so the club said that they would have to withdraw completely from their league and competitive rugby in Ireland, unless the IRFU changed their policy towards the wearing of goggles.

Each of these campaigns received significant media support and were very important for the overall campaign in Ireland. Indeed, other players and parents shared their experiences with me, from which Cords was able to compile a database of affected players for the IRFU.

Our direct engagement with the IRFU began in July 2015, when we wrote to them about their position and, at our request, Philip and I arranged to meet Dr Rod McLoughlin, the Union's director of medical services, on July 6th, 2015 in the IRFU headquarters on Lansdowne Road, to discuss the Union's reservations about the goggles.

The meeting lasted about an hour. Dr McLoughlin outlined his medical concerns with the goggles, including the risk of skin abrasions. As neither Philip or I were medically qualified to answer these points nor was there any conclusive research available at that stage to counter his specific concerns, we felt the need to take some of the points away and work out means to respond more authoritatively.

A significant aspect of the research at that time came from the experience of players such as myself. Therefore, we felt that the IRFU's reservations appeared to be based on medical interpretation, rather than hard, conclusive research. Ultimately, we found Dr McLoughlin to be very cautious and he didn't really give much away in the meeting. However, meeting him at least served to plant a seed in his mind and helped us to understand the presenting issues.

For my second season with Viadana, 2015-16, I was made captain. Once again, we finished just outside the play-offs and I was nominated for player of the championship, and finished second again. But early in the season, on the last weekend of September 2015 during the World Cup, Viadana informed me that Zebre wanted me as a permit player, meaning I could cover for Zebre when their international players were away.

At the time, I lived in Parma so the Stadio Sergio Lanfranchi and Zebre's training base was a five-minute drive for me, and actually easier than driving to Viadana, which sometimes could take up to 40 minutes. I knew I had a good chance of being involved in the squad the following week as Zebre had so many players at the World Cup. It was a thrill to train with players like Luke Burgess, the former Australian scrum-half, and the legendary All Blacks' full-back Mils Muliaina.

The Italian Union were one of the first to sign up to the trial, which meant I could play with Zebre, but only in home games. On October 4th, 2015 I played for Zebre against the Scarlets in Parma, bridging a four-year gap since my last game in the Pro12, meaning it was the first time the goggles had been seen in that competition. My previous appearance had been for Leinster against Glasgow in May, 2011. The sun was shining. I felt great. I had been training and playing really well, so I was all set for a good performance. They had a scrum in their 22 and as the water carriers were leaving the field, one of their guys just stared at me and kept staring. "A bit weird looking aren't they?" I said because he couldn't take his eyes off me. I knew this was going to happen plenty.

In the next round, a fortnight later, Zebre wanted me to play in their Pro12 game against Connacht in Galway. A week beforehand, on October 9th, 2015, I wrote to the IRFU seeking clarification on their position and to ask if I would be allowed to play for Zebre against Connacht at the Sportsground.

Four hours later their response was not the one I wanted. If I played the game, I would be in breach of Regulation 12 and the IRFU would be open to sanction.

To play the game, I was offered this solution: 'A player from a participating Union may not wear goggles while playing in the jurisdiction of a Union who does not wish to participate in the Trial.'

Given I was gouged twice, I was not going to play without my goggles. This was the moment to go public and fight my situation based on three issues:

1) The IRFU's stance was a breach of my rights under the Irish Constitution and under the European Convention of Human Rights law based on disability.

2) It was a breach of my freedom of travel to provide services pursuant to EU law, and also a breach of the European Charter of Fundamental Rights.

3) There was no legal impact but their stance contradicted the "Spirit of Rugby" slogan that all unions aspire to achieve.

That night, with me on Skype, my entire family sat down for hours and we devised a strategy for breaking the deadlock with the IRFU. With the Connacht v Zebre match fast approaching on Friday 16th October, we had to act quickly in order to raise awareness of the problem.

My sister Emma had worked in communications for the ISPCC and Children's Rights Alliance, so she was able to connect me with a communications expert, Martina Quinn from Alice PR. Martina agreed to come on board our campaign and set about devising a superb media strategy.

We also sought advice from a professor of law, with a specialism in sports law, Neville Cox on how to proceed. Neville is now the Registrar of Trinity College Dublin. His advice proved invaluable.

On October 13th I wrote to the heads of World Rugby and the IRFU requesting that the goggle trial be ended so that they could come into law, thus permitting me and others to continue our career, and our passion. But as things stood, the legality of where I could use them was an issue for clubs who played in European competitions. We decided to launch a campaign to have the goggles permitted in the game's laws.

Paul O'Connell had suffered a torn hamstring the previous Sunday, October 11th, in the deciding World Cup pool win over France in Cardiff and Ireland were preparing for their quarter-final against Argentina the following Sunday, so we needed to be smart.

Even so, on October 15th, the "Let Ian Play" campaign was launched along with a press release highlighting how I wasn't being allowed to play with the goggles the following day in Galway.

The campaign started early with an interview on 'Morning Ireland' on RTÉ Radio 1 with Des Cahill and also an article in the Irish Times. Soon the story featured in Irish, English and Italian newspapers, blogs, podcasts and radio stations and even on RTÉ's famous Joe Duffy Radio Show.

Letters were written to ministers and politicians and our press release prompted a host of interviews. My phone was hopping and we had 10,000 signatures in 24 hours, which then rose steadily to almost 15,000 signatures over a ten-day period. My case had clearly struck a nerve.

On the day Connacht were hosting Zebre, Friday October 16th, Philip organised a gathering at the Sportsground to help generate more signatures. He arrived at the stadium with Dad and a few people he knew, including his school friend Charlie Langley, equipped with t-shirts and a giant "Let Ian Play" banner. Philip was interviewed on Galway Bay FM about the protest. A large number of fans attending the game expressed their emphatic support. I made players from both teams aware of my brother's efforts and they posed for a picture after the game wearing the t-shirts in support of the campaign.

Some of my old Irish Under-20s teammates played for Connacht and wanted to support the campaign, but we learned that this was frowned upon by some in the IRFU, as the players were taking a stance against their employers. Hence, the photo we ended up publishing had to be the one without those Connacht players.

Media coverage of our campaign became global. I was inundated with messages of support, including from former Irish rugby internationals and, surprisingly, by some very senior people within the game. The flood of goodwill, especially from unexpected quarters, was extremely encouraging.

A number of people also offered me their assistance, including Martin O'Brien, an optometrist in Enniscorthy, Co Wexford. Martin was an executive member of the Association of Optometrists of Ireland and the Irish representative of the European Council of Optometry and Optics. His Irish and European perspectives proved absolutely vital for the campaign.

Minutes after the Connacht match had ended, I received an email response from World Rugby. It definitely wasn't the warmest or most encouraging of letters I have ever received. I was told that all unions are autonomous and can choose to be part of the trial or not. They stated that the trial would hopefully finish by the end of 2016, two years after it started. That would be a fifth change in the date for completion of the trial.

The pressure was increasing as Zebre wanted to sign me for cover during the Six Nations as well but, with games away to

Leinster and Ulster in this window, it would be impossible for them to sign me if I wasn't permitted to play by the IRFU. They and I needed to know urgently!

With more and more stories of underage players wishing to use goggles beginning to surface, we genuinely explored the possibility of setting up a Goggles Players Association.

On October 19th, Philip contacted Jon Trenge, an American wrestler who used goggles due to a detached retina, which happened when he competed in the NCAA championship. We even considered contacting the Dutch footballer Edgar Davids, but his issue was Glaucoma.

Finally, we had something of a breakthrough when, on November 2nd, I received special dispensation from the RFU for future cross-border games in England. I had initially contacted them a week prior to their response, and they were very accommodating. In fact, they endorsed and welcomed any further initiatives with the goggles.

I wrote to the IRFU again on November 4th, explaining that I had opportunities to sign for clubs bigger than Viadana, but I couldn't do anything until this issue was resolved. Two days later I was told that the issue would be brought up at the IRFU Medical Committee meeting towards the end of the month. Hearing this, I submitted a request to the Union that I be allowed to make a presentation in person in support of the goggles.

I also contacted IRUPA, the players union, on November 9th.

As a former Irish player, they took me on as one of their own and were extremely supportive. They informed me that the Medical Committee meeting would take place on December 16th at 6pm at the IRFU offices. My request to attend was granted, but only for a ten-minute presentation. My whole support network needed to accumulate as much information as possible to make the case on behalf of the goggles impossible to turn down.

Despite the invitation to attend the Medical Committee meeting in early December to discuss the trial, on Monday 23rd November the IRFU released a "GOGGLES Q&A" to every Honorary Secretary in every rugby club in Ireland outlining the reasons why they were not entering the trial. They requested each club to circulate the contents widely. It appeared at that stage that the IRFU were digging their heels in.

However, the following day, Tuesday 24th November the front page of the Irish Times sport section, featured the headline, 'IRFU stance on goggles doesn't make sense, say eye experts'. The Association of Optometrists of Ireland had held their AGM at the beginning of November and passed a motion to support the goggles. This information had not been formally publicised. A letter had been drafted to send to the IRFU, to encourage them to sign up to the trial, but it hadn't yet been sent. However, the IRFU's circular to clubs proved a timely moment and Martin O'Brien was interviewed as an eye expert to give his opinion as a member of the national body which oversees protective eyewear.

I understand that this article caused significant consternation, however it was a huge boost to the campaign to have the full support of the main national body of eyewear professionals in Ireland.

By now, "Team McKinley" was a well-oiled machine. We would either meet at the family home in Whitechurch, with me on Skype, or have Skype meetings or email chains that would go on for page after page. Everyone did their part. It was almost like detective work.

Cords set up a survey on who would need or support the goggles around the island of Ireland. Dad was brilliant on the tactical side of things and also in utilising his many rugby contacts. Philip and Emma knew plenty of people and their attitude was: 'Well, if you don't ask you don't get.' Because it was close to Christmas time, Mum was on Christmas pudding duty for all the people that helped but she was crucial in obtaining some of the contacts. Andrew was able to support all of us emotionally as it was a very stressful time.

On Friday 27th November Dad and Philip had a very positive meeting with the former Olympic silver medalist and then Chief Executive of the Irish Sports Council, John Treacy, and his colleague Colm McGinty in the Sport Ireland office in Blanchardstown, West Dublin.

Around about this same time, Dad spoke to Pa Whelan, who was at that time the IRFU rep on World Rugby. This was all part of a process of keeping the pressure on those bodies most directly connected to my case, in the hope of a satisfactory resolution.

Dad also took the personal initiative at the time of having a private meeting with a very senior and respected figure in Irish rugby about my whole case and the continuing blockage to it being experienced from the IRFU.

A couple of days before the meeting with the Medical Committee, we sent the IRFU our counter arguments, with different pieces of evidence in favour of the goggles against their independent ophthalmologist's findings, which were founded many months before the finished goggles became available. Our submission included letters from the top ophthalmologists in the country and the consultant plastic surgeon Dr Siún Murphy supporting the safety of rugby goggles, as well as a letter from an insurance company which showed that I was not covered to play in games without the goggles and letters from elite clubs stating they could not sign me if I wasn't permitted to play in those countries that had not signed up to the trial.

It also included some of the media coverage which had been generated by the campaign, results from our survey regarding visual impairment within rugby in Ireland, and letters of support from other people in a similar situation to mine including Disability Sport Northern Ireland. We also had presentations by Raleri on the making of the goggles, John Merrigan's design project and Eli Peli's field expansion project.

Come December 16th, I booked a flight from Milan into

Dublin for a one-night stay. Philip was working in DCU (Dublin City University), so he was close to the airport and picked me up that afternoon. We went to his office and went over my ten-minute presentation which he had drafted after all the information had been gathered by the family. I re-read it until I knew it blindfolded.

•••••

Before going to the IRFU offices just beside Lansdowne Road I changed into my old navy Leinster suit, and an old IRFU tie, to show that I was once part of their system. As we neared the offices, I became more and more nervous. It hit me that this wasn't just for me. The hopes of plenty of other people were riding on this meeting, so my delivery needed to be right. I was also confident though because I knew I was fighting for a just cause. I had researched the make-up of the board and funnily enough I knew three of them. An IRUPA representative would also be in attendance and able to speak in support of my campaign. I was asked to sit outside the boardroom and wait to be called in, but this was going to be the first item discussed on the agenda.

When I was called in, the first thing I did was shake the hands of the people I knew and look them straight in the eye. The floor was mine. I started my ten-minute presentation by thanking the committee for their time. However, before I made my presentation, I informed them that firstly I had to address something, namely a journalist being contacted late at night by someone close to the IRFU during the goggles campaign who claimed I was motivated by business interests with the Italian manufacturers Raleri.

Quite the contrary, I said. I was not a shareholder, financial investor or business accomplice in any form. I paid for my flights back to Ireland for meetings such as this one, as well as that trip to Boston to develop field expansion further, not to mention simply paying for the goggles themselves. In fact, I was out of pocket because of them. I said this claim was hugely insulting.

After that, the presentation could not have gone any smoother and I felt like I was walking on cloud nine as I left. I believe that we had amounted far more evidence in support of the campaign, whereas the IRFU appeared to rely on the opinion of one person, who was not named. I still have a letter from the IRFU saying I can play without the goggles but I cannot play with them (which, of course, would have been far more dangerous). The reasons they presented were insurance and safety but I believe we countered each of their concerns very well.

During my presentation, most of the board members didn't make any eye contact with me, they just looked down at their table as I spoke which indicated to me that this was going only one way. Philip was waiting eagerly for me outside and he sensed it went well simply because we had prepared so exhaustively. I gave him a massive hug when I got back to the car.

Two days later, December 18th, I was in my apartment in Parma when an email from the IRFU pinged into my inbox. It stated that the Union would be requesting that they be part of the rugby goggles trial.

YES!

David v Goliath and David wins again! There it was in black and white:

"IRFU TO APPLY FOR PARTICIPATION IN WORLD RUGBY RALERI GOGGLES TRIAL."

We arranged a "Team McKinley" meeting that night and I thanked all my family for their hard work. It was a huge, landmark day for everyone involved, and everyone who had supported us.

Later we heard through IRUPA that the meeting had lasted four hours and that the legal implications appeared to have been discussed the most.

On December 22nd, I was able to return to Ireland again and feature with seven-year-old rugby player Ryan Totten from Coleraine on BBC Radio with an early Christmas present for him, namely a pair of the goggles.

The following February, Zebre called me in for another home match, against Leinster – my first game against my old province. The weather was beautiful all week but, of course, come the day of the match, Parma had to be hit with one of the biggest downpours of the year. That made things more difficult. I played okay. Kicked five points. But a Leinster team featuring Tadhg Furlong, Ross

Molony, my old mate Dominic Ryan, Dan Leavy, Luke McGrath, Garry Ringrose and Isa Nacewa was too strong.

My third game for Zebre was on March 4th 2016, against Ulster in Belfast, which was a landmark day for the goggles as it was the first time they featured in a match sanctioned by the IRFU.

Our captain that day, Marco Bortolami, ran onto the Kingspan Stadium holding the hands of my two nephews, Matthew and Nathan McKinley. I came on as a substitute for the second half.

The Irish campaign was now complete. Ireland had become the first Union to change their mind and sign up to the Global Law trial.

Now we needed to work on England and France so that goggles could be worn worldwide.

•••••

English campaign (RFU) 2015

Like Ireland, the primary impetus for England's goggle campaign came from underage rugby. While my story did receive some interest in the English papers, in November 2013 a Darlington nine-year-old named Adam Clayton featured prominently after he was barred from playing rugby whilst wearing his recently purchased, expensive Rx goggles.

Following this, the England Rugby Union (RFU) contacted the Association of British Dispensing Opticians (the British equivalent of the Association of Optometrists of Ireland) to explore solutions. Although we were already in deep discussions with the IRB about designs at that time, the RFU decided to go it alone and set up their own independent, national Under-13s trial. They were unhappy with the one-size fits all designs which the IRB were developing.

In April 2014, the Norville Group in Gloucester therefore developed what it called the Progear Tackle Goggle for use in the RFU trial.

In some ways there were some positives with this, in that the RFU, unlike the IRFU and FFR, were at least willing to permit some goggle use in England. However, as an adult I could not participate in their particular trial. It was also positive that the RFU were working alongside the key eyecare professionals, unlike the IRFU.

However, the disadvantage of the RFU's actions from my perspective, was that it served to counteract and even undermine the IRB/Raleri goggles trial and that it was one Union acting unilaterally without wider cooperation.

In many ways, as an adult and with such an unusual case, my needs were not at the forefront of any of these considerations. Therefore, I wrote to Ian Ritchie, the CEO of the RFU in October 2015 and he sent me a really helpful and encouraging reply on November 2nd which stated the RFU's interpretation of their legal position. They believed that as a visiting player, registered in a country which was participating in the trial, that I could play in England for matches as part of international competitions. However, if I wished to join an English-based club, then I would not be permitted to play with Raleri goggles. This seemed a really pragmatic and sensible solution and one which Ian Ritchie reinforced in a formal letter in July 2016.

This letter ultimately assisted me in securing a professional contract with Benetton Treviso.

So, while I didn't get RFU to sign up to the World Rugby goggles trial, I was able to secure a local arrangement to allow me to play in England for European competitions. I was also glad that a mechanism was available for underage players to access some form of protective eyewear.

On Saturday 24th October 2016, a week after the sudden death of Anthony Foley, I found myself lined out for Benetton Treviso against Gloucester in Kingsholm Stadium standing for a minute's silence for the Munster legend, in front of a packed house for my first Challenge Cup match on English soil. We were facing some big names that day, such as James Hook, Greig Laidlaw and Jonny May on the wing. The raucous, up-close crowd also gave me plenty of comments about my goggles that day.

While the RFU's trial was supposed to last just one season – 2014-15 – it only concluded in 2019, during which time 250 players took part in it. Following the full adoption of World

Rugby's goggles in 2019, it is my understanding that both the Norville and Raleri goggles are currently approved for use in England, an anomaly in international rugby.

French campaign (FFR) 2016

The last Union to change their stance was the French Federation.

Former French Under-20s international and Perpignan scrum-half, Florian Cazenave, was the most high profile figure in France to campaign for rugby goggles. His story had received significant coverage in French media. However, in 2016 he was like me, based in Italy and campaigning from afar.

On June 15th, 2016, a meeting took place with World Rugby in Dublin to push the GLT (Global Law Trial). Myself, my dad and Philip were all in attendance. World Rugby was represented by Mark Harrington (Head of Technical Services) and Marc Douglas (Technical Services).

We argued that the goggles had been approved for a trial by the Italian Federation but not the French Federation. So as part of our submission we cited the ridiculous example of being able to play for Treviso against Toulon in the Champions Cup in Italy one week but the next week not being permitted to play for Italy in France because the FFR were not a part of this trial. World Rugby confirmed this was the case.

Following the meeting there were letters back and forth with the former English rugby captain and President of World

Rugby, Sir Bill Beaumont. He was helpful in his engagement but seemed somewhat powerless to force the FFR's hand.

While the French Federation stalled, I lost out on experience and on money. I felt discriminated against. We looked into European Law. My sister is very good on that stuff.

We were told that World Rugby's deadline for the trial would be pushed back to September 2017. That was too late for me. I would become eligible for Italy in January 2017, and I couldn't have a situation where I could not be picked simply because I wasn't allowed to play on a certain union's turf.

So, on July 16th, we sent a translated French letter to the French Federation, the FFR, explaining my situation, much like we did with the IRFU the previous December. The difference was I didn't receive a response, even to my follow-up letter! It just so happened that Benetton were drawn in the same pool as two French teams in our Challenge Cup group, namely La Rochelle and Bayonne. As this meant I wasn't permitted to play in those away games, I needed to have this resolved. My situation was ridiculous.

There was now plenty of correspondence with World Rugby and, on December 2nd, 2016, I received a letter in French from the FFR saying that I had to provide the insurance indemnity myself in order to play Challenge Cup games in France. This potentially could have involved a significant sum of money.

The letter was written by the then FFR President, Monsieur Pierre Camou, whom sources suggested was the stumbling block on this issue. Remarkably, the following day, 3rd December, Mr Camou was elected out of office and replaced by the former Champions Cup and Six Nations winning coach, Bernard Laporte. Monsieur Camou's letter to me, possibly marked one of his last acts in office.

We had actually been following the election campaign with some interest for quite a while. During the summer of 2016, Bernard Laporte had visited Pau for a town hall rally as part of his election campaign. Following a question from a rugby player with an eye disability, Laporte stated that he would support goggles if elected.

True to his word, during his acceptance speech the new FFR President declared that he was in favour of the goggles and that the FFR would seek to join the World Rugby trial. The following day marked my 27th birthday.

One of the issues which had been raised a number of times, in various ways by the FFR throughout our campaign, was the claim that their medical regulations had to be approved by the French Sport Ministry. In other words, the FFR had been shifting the blame onto their government. However, Laporte's declaration at his acceptance speech, seemed to make a mockery of this stance. It suggested that the blockage must have lay with the previous FFR President all along.

Yet, despite all these dramatic and sudden developments, after six months of negotiations in preparation for this scenario, a full resolution for my participation was still not in sight only a few days out from Benetton's Challenge Cup game away to Bayonne on Friday, December 9th.

Matchday squads are picked early in the week, and I was due to be involved, but Benetton had to place me on a special insurance plan for the game.

Two days before the game, and a day before we were to travel to France, I received special dispensation from the FFR to play in games in France for the upcoming season. The opposition clubs were satisfied, so were World Rugby, the FFR and the EPCR.

Come kick-off in Bayonne, I'd already won. Even so, I was named on the bench, and that's where I stayed. I was never brought on, which really irritated me after all the hard work which went into obtaining my clearance, all the more so as that night, in the south-west of France, Benetton won their first away game in European competition in nine years. I was so pissed off.

The goggles did make their debut on French soil in the same competition on January 21st, 2017, when I started against La Rochelle. By then, the French Federation had signed up to the trial and, on December 29th, Florian Cazenave, signed for Brive for the following season, 2017-18, in the Top14.

France had finally fallen, bringing an end to our exhausting threefold campaign.

I could finally focus my energies on being a professional rugby player and not a full-time lobbyist. In many ways though, the best campaigning I could do for the goggles now, was to simply play well with them week after week and to raise their profile within the highest levels of the game.

That said, the goggles remained under "trial". If, at any point, World Rugby said they were no longer trialling the goggles, I would have had to stop playing. So, we continued to hound World Rugby, as still there were discrepancies between jurisdictions under different unions.

I suspect World Rugby never fully believed that any player could play at international level with these goggles. Nor did they maybe appreciate just how much of a fight I and my family were prepared to make.

However, finally, on May 28th, 2019, World Rugby approved the use of the goggles in rugby globally, bringing an end to the Global Law Trial that had started in 2014.

Rugby goggles were legal.

It had only taken five years.

TEN

Rebuilding

WHEN I look back on my second game for Zebre, against Leinster during the 2016 Six Nations, I prepared for it in completely the wrong way. I had been too uptight and nervous, and this definitely affected how I played.

The fantastic weather of that week in February 2016 gave way to torrential rain in Parma on matchday. The pitch was like a bog. All I remember from before the game was lying in my bedroom with my legs up against the wall and feeling physically sick with nerves. I couldn't even eat any of my lunch.

This was entirely because I was about to play against Leinster and once the match kicked off I just tried too hard basically. This was my first game against my ex-teammates and the guys I grew up with, but I didn't embrace the occasion.

With Benetton, playing against the Irish provinces, and especially Leinster, became second nature. In my first season there I played against all four Irish provinces, both home and away. Whenever they came over to Treviso, I would drop a message to some of the guys I knew to see if they wanted to meet up for a coffee. Prior to that Zebre-Leinster game I didn't do that.

Aside from the conditions and losing 27-10, I remember being shouted at all day by the Leinster centre Ben Te'o. Whenever we had the ball he was constantly in my ear: "I've got the 'Goggles.'" Isa Nacewa also gave me an almighty tackle. I honestly thought I had cracked ribs. They weren't right for weeks.

Still, it had been nice having some food and a brief chat after the game with guys I played with like Dominic Ryan, Noel Reid, Jordi Murphy and the strength and conditioning coach Dan Tobin, who had done so much with me in my years in the academy, before they flew home that evening on a charter flight.

At least I applied some of those lessons the following week away to Ulster. My preparations were in complete contrast. I knew that it was going to be my last game for Zebre as a permit player before the international players came back from Six Nations duty.

This was a chance to embrace the game for what it was and also to play in Ireland again after all the lobbying and fighting off the pitch.

I thoroughly enjoyed that week. Away games were not Zebre's priority – they shipped 70 points in Glasgow – and we lost this one 32-0. But I knew that other teams were looking at me and I resolved to play as best as I could, which I did after coming on at half-time after Edoardo Padovani suffered a broken hand. My whole family were there to see me play for the first time since my Leinster days and, although it sounds weird after a 32-0 defeat, I probably played one of my better games that season in those 40 minutes. I felt very comfortable and happy that the goggles stood up against frontline professionals. That gave me a sense of satisfaction.

About three months later, near the end of May, my agent and I met with Benetton Rugby to finalise my contract for the upcoming season.

They'd just had their worst ever season, winning three and losing 19 matches to finish bottom of the Pro12, missing out on qualification for the Champions Cup to Zebre on the last day.

I knew that Kieran Crowley had already been announced as the new head coach after eight years in charge of the Canadian national team. He'd had a distinguished career with the All Blacks, competing in two World Cups and earning a winner's medal from the very first World Cup in 1987. He had even been to a Benetton game towards the end of the season. In addition to a new coaching ticket, the whole squad was being completely revamped. Out of 40 players nearly 15 were leaving, including three out-halves, with a similar number coming in. A new culture was growing in the club.

I had no hesitation in meeting them. My agent had told me that other clubs had been interested before, even in my first season with Viadana, but I had no interest in leaving Italy. By then I had come to love the Italian way of life and had become fixated on the idea of rebuilding my career there.

Treviso, or Benetton as it is now known, is traditionally a big rugby club which was at its lowest ebb, but that almost meant you were going in there without anything to lose. When you finish last, the only way is up. Yet I also firmly believed that something very positive was going to be built there under Kieran and the club had the potential to become something more.

Historically the town of Treviso is a point of reference in a sporting context for Italy. Volleyball, basketball and rugby have all dominated domestic competitions. Even the local football team was promoted into Serie A in 2005. The Benetton family were major backers of sport in Treviso and this included the rugby team. Luciano, one of the co-founders of Benetton who also served as an Italian senator, had a huge interest in Italian rugby and was very keen to see Benetton succeed.

We eventually met Kieran and Antonio Pavanello, who used to play in the Italian second-row and spent over a decade at Benetton, and was now their Sporting Director, in the offices of La Ghirada, the club's training complex in Treviso. 'Pava' talked about my Man of the Match performance for Leinster against Benetton in 2011 but obviously this was now 2016 so time had moved on and I was now playing with the goggles.

It was my first time meeting Kieran and he was very straight to the point in talking about my goal-kicking and my percentages, and what was expected of me as an out-half. This was good as it gave me clear directions about what the team needed from me. The meeting went well and I signed a one-year contract with the option of a second year. I was delighted.

That brought an end to our two-year stay in Parma, where we had eventually moved into a two-bedroom, two-bathroom, top floor apartment on the sixth floor. My dad always reminded me that there were 96 steps to reach it because there was no elevator. It possibly wouldn't have passed many Fire and Safety tests as there were no fire exits either.

It was an old apartment block close to the train station. Thankfully it had air conditioning, which wasn't commonplace in the older buildings, and that helped alleviate the searing temperatures in summertime.

Cordelia came over and we went to job agencies to find work for her. Although her Italian had inevitably become a little rusty after a year and a half in London, she soon began picking it up again. She became a private English teacher for various companies around the area, going from place to place on her bike as we only had one car and she was a little apprehensive about driving on the other side of the road. If possible I picked her up after training, but she was really satisfied with what she was doing there.

Parma, which is in the Emilia-Romagna region and quite central in the north of Italy, is most famous for its cuisine, being close to Modena and its balsamic vinegar, as well as a Ferrari factory. It has a very flat terrain whereas many Italian towns have a landmark to it, be it the mountains, the sea or architecture. The coast was an hour and a half's drive away.

There are lovely parts of Parma, including the cathedral. Whenever family or friends would come to visit we took them to beautiful castles on the outskirts of the city. But mostly people go there for a cuisine experience, and we were treated to very good food most of the time.

It's also home to one of the oldest universities in the world and, as well as the rugby club, a football club that had long been established in Serie A even though the Stadio Ennio Tardini is not one of Italy's mega stadiums. It has always remained fairly humble, with a capacity of not much more than 25,000. The club also ran into financial difficulties and, in 2015, was declared bankrupt, which led to a new club being re-founded and starting off life in Serie D. Parma Calcio returned to Serie A with three successive promotions but are now in Serie B.

The great goalkeeper Gianluigi Buffon started his career there and is now back in Parma, where he is contracted until 2024, when he will be 46.

Historically, rugby has always been big in Parma and dates back to the foundation of the city's first club in 1931. That's why one of Italy's two professional teams are based in Zebre, or Zebre Parma as they have been rebranded. There have been three different rugby clubs in Parma, including mergers, and when the Excellenza was really big the Parma teams were often prominent. In fact, Crociati Parma Rugby won the title three times in the '50s. Most of Italy's wealth is concentrated in the north, and the Parma clubs would have been well funded.

Rugby players enjoy living there. It's very relaxed although one negative for me was that you would have to drive quite a distance to visit places or do things.

I only played two home games for Zebre at the Stadio Sergio Lanfranchi, a nice 5,000-seat capacity ground that is the perfect size for the Parma rugby community.

Only the derbies against Benetton would fill the ground, usually at Christmas time or the last day of the season, and whenever it was full the atmosphere was brilliant. The apartment we had in Parma was very close to the stadium, and they have been restructuring it with a built-in gym and club house.

But on the pitch they have struggled. In the 2021-22 URC season they won one match and lost 17 in finishing last. They have some good young players but it is difficult when many of the relatively older and experienced guys in their late 20s have stepped away. It is a tough situation.

I would go back to the Lanfranchi and play for Benetton three times, and it was one of my favourite pitches to play on. The Lanfranchi has those classically traditional back and white Italian posts. I never missed a kick, funnily enough, on that pitch.

As well as being a very nice place to live, Parma was quite a culinary experience, but we definitely felt more at home in Treviso. Parma was quite isolated and for a flight to Ireland you would have to drive to Milan, which was a good 90 minutes away.

Not only does Treviso have an airport which was five minutes from our apartment, but there are also direct flights to and from Ireland, so we never felt as far away or as disconnected from families and friends. We also had Venice airport 30 minutes away.

Benetton had a high intensity, three-week bloc in pre-season and my apartment wasn't ready until after that, in July, so I had to room with one of my teammates for that period. Then I came back to Ireland, had a two-week break, and returned to Treviso with Cordelia.

Finding an apartment was easier in Treviso because the club had someone to do that for you. I travelled there twice, once with Cordelia, to look at apartments they offered us. Again, we picked a top floor apartment, on the fifth floor this time, but at least it had an elevator, so it seemed like paradise. Carrying your shopping up 96 steps is not ideal, and if you leave something in the car you have to renegotiate those 96 steps down and up again.

The location for us was perfect because it was near to the airport, the Stadio Monigo and our La Ghirada training base. Furthermore, it was just a ten-minute walk from the town centre.

There was a good mixture of people living on the fifth floor. An elderly couple, whom we still stay in touch with, were almost like grandparents to us. Her name is Clara and she took us under her wing. She made tiramisu (which is said to have originated in Treviso) and other traditional Italian treats and left them in a plastic bag at the door for us. If she saw our post box was full, she would take our post up for us, and if we went away she cleaned our bins, even though I never asked her to do so. She looked after us very well. Almost too well.

Treviso is known as 'Little Venice' and we both fell in love with the place instantaneously.

It is a good size, about 70-80,000 people, and it has pretty much everything you would want. The centre is within 14th century Venetian walls (le Mura) with entry through four different gates and Treviso had a real sense of being a family-orientated city. Like anywhere else we lived in Italy, it is home to a classical Italian lifestyle with people sitting outside, but because it is much more compact, this way of life seemed more obvious.

The elderly men would be sitting outside bars drinking their spritzers and reading the newspapers and soaking up the sunshine. There always seemed to be food markets somewhere and every Saturday morning there was a wide variety of clothes markets.

Venice was just half an hour away by train, and you couldn't find a more romantic place for an evening meal. I'll always remember that the train ticket was a mere €3.30.

There are plenty of cycling trails too, but my main hobby

while living there was cooking. I absolutely loved it and Cordelia arranged cooking courses for me.

Prosecco originated in Treviso and there's no better place to learn about wine making than in the spectacular Prosecco Hills. Cordelia was always into wine, having worked in an O'Brien's off-licence and also for a wine PR company in London, and I followed suit living in Italy. It sounds a bit cheesy, in every sense, but we went to agriturismos, which were literally country villas, and tasted wine with their cheese and meat platters. Some of my teammates owned boats so I was taken on day trips by water to Venice, or some of the islands around Venice.

We also continued to attend Italian classes in a little university in Treviso. It was an all-in investment. Cordelia's Italian improved significantly. She never thought it was any good but whenever family or friends came over, they always said: "Wow, you can speak Italian."

Parma has a cathedral and a famous tower, the Battistero di Parma, which are quintessential to the city, whereas Treviso doesn't have a big cathedral or church, but it is an untapped city. There are little cafés which overlook the canals, some of which run under the city. One restaurant we particularly liked to visit has a glass floor with the canals washing away underneath your feet.

We also had the Dolomites nearby, where Benetton did their pre-season training. That was pretty special. One of the places we visited in the Dolomites was Cortina d'Ampezzo, a summer and winter sport resort which hosted the 1956 Winter Olympics and had all the slaloms and slopes.

Being something of a traditional rugby town is also rare in Italy. Different bars had rugby memorabilia with, say, a Treviso jersey or a framed photograph of the Treviso team of 1995. If you went to Udine or Parma, there might be some advertising for the upcoming game, but any of the bars with a sports' theme were devoted to the Udine or Parma football teams.

After pre-season games against a Bernard Jackman-coached Grenoble side and a Leicester team featuring the likes of Manu Tuilagi, Tom Youngs and Ellis Genge, my Benetton debut was in their first Pro12 game of the season against Leinster in the RDS in September 2016. There was no getting away from them.

I'll always remember when I came on in the 60th minute. There was a massive cheer and a standing ovation, and I'm very grateful to those people but, ultimately, we lost 20-8. My family were all at the game and celebrated the occasion by wearing "Forza McKinley" t-shirts with my image on them.

I was taken aback by the applause from the crowd and that meant an awful lot to me. I didn't want to receive a sympathetic cheer and it certainly sounded to me like it was a positive and enthusiastic one instead. There was a reset scrum when I came on which gave me some time to compose myself after that ovation and that helped me refocus on the game in front of me.

Joey Carbery marked his Leinster debut with two tries. He scored one from about 50 metres and ran around our full-back Jayden Hayward. Jayden was very quick, but Joey made him look slow. Joey was very, very good that day. He looked an exciting prospect, a player who could play what was in front of him and had all the tools to do so. A red-hot talent.

To be honest that season was a bit of a slog although towards the end you felt that something was changing in players' attitudes and what Kieran was trying to implement was starting to happen.

We were going in the right direction. We beat the Ospreys (13-5) and Edinburgh (21-6) at home in the run-in, and this was after shipping a 64-10 defeat away to the Ospreys the previous September.

So, over the course of the season we made modest improvements, winning five games, and three of our last five, to finish tenth and secured Champions Cup qualification on the last day of the season when we beat Zebre in Parma.

The two Italian sides went into that final game level on points and the Stadio Sergio Lanfranchi was bouncing with a 4,500 capacity. I started our last nine games of the season at out-half and kicked 14 points in that 19-3 win over Zebre. Although it was May, the rain was pissing down in Parma and playing in goggles in those conditions was never easy.

However, Cordelia would always say to me: "You play your best rugby in the rain" so I told myself to take the game by the scruff of the neck.

Pin the corners. Do what I would do on a wet day in Ireland.

REBUILDING

Playing in St Columba's you always had the mountain wind coming down from Kilmashogue into a particular corner and it would usually be wet, so I tried to tap into my boyhood memories. Philip also came over for the game and was there with Cordelia.

Zebre's out-half, Carlo Canna, was in the Italian squad with my Benetton teammate Tommaso Allan during the Six Nations until Tommy was injured, and was the Azzurri's first-choice '10'. Hence, he was in my sights and I knew Conor O'Shea, the Italian head coach, was in the crowd. It was a good team effort and we won pretty convincingly.

I played 26 games in all that season, starting 16 of them, and was an unused sub in the other two, so I was involved in every game despite playing with a shoulder injury from about mid-way through. That perhaps also highlighted the thinness of our squad. I was pretty tired at the end of the season but I was also thrilled because I had been involved in every matchday squad.

Marty Banks, one of the other out-halves, had been due to arrive for that season but instead joined for the 2017-18 campaign, so ultimately myself and Tommy Allan were the out-halves for the whole season. This showed not only that my body could stand up to it, but so too could the goggles.

The morning after the Zebre game, myself, Cordelia and Philip were having breakfast in the University quarter of Treviso when I had a phone call from Conor.

He said: "Well done yesterday. You're in the squad but you won't be travelling."

This was in reference to Italy's summer tour to Singapore, where they played Scotland, before going on to Fiji and Australia. I had been named in the wider 44-man squad but Conor warned me that I would not be in the travelling squad of 31 players. I felt like I was in contention because I'd been playing so well but I accepted his decision. The fact he called me so soon after the game was a good sign as well that I was getting closer to being picked and it reinforced in my mind that I had to just keep going and keep improving.

Although Italy had lost all five games in the Six Nations, Carlo had been the starting out-half when Italy beat South Africa the previous November. Understandably, that can hold a huge amount of weight.

But I was closer than ever to breaking into the Italian team.

Things were going in the right direction.

And my main objective for the 2017-18 season was pretty clearcut.

ELEVEN

The Azzurri

I BECAME eligible for Italy through the three-year residency rule in January 2017. If I was registered when I first arrived in Italy, I would have been eligible for the 2015 World Cup, which goes to show that when I first moved over my intentions were not to play again.

The process had begun with Leonorso in January 2014 when I went to the local university for a medical and the paperwork was started by the club, and about a month before I became eligible for Italy, I contacted Conor O'Shea to arrange a meeting.

I sat down with Conor at Benetton's training centre La Ghirada in the coaches' office, just to see where I stood in his thinking and what I needed to do if I was to be part of his plans and break into the Italian team. It was four years since I'd moved to Italy and on one level it was just nice to talk to somebody from Ireland about Italian rugby. We cut to the chase soon enough though because I'd called for the meeting with one purpose in mind; finding out exactly what I had to do to impress Conor enough to become part of his plans for the Italy team. To his credit, he was pretty up front with me about what he wanted me to work on. My kicking game needed to improve and my percentages needed to improve off the tee. But that focused the mind even more.

Before the 2017-18 season, another major event happened in my life as Cordelia and I were married at my in-laws' Richard and Rosalind's wedding venue, Ballyscullion Park, in Bellaghy in Northern Ireland – Seamus Heaney country.

The venue had only been in existence for a few years and as this was the first time one of their children was getting married it was obviously a special time for them. We had a lovely day and it didn't rain, which is always a bonus in Ireland.

I'd say there were about 160 or so at the wedding, in addition to old friends and schoolmates, there was a mixture of guys from Leinster, Udine, Viadana and Benetton. Because I had been bouncing all over the place in my rugby career I picked up friends in various places. My best man was my best friend, Andrew Lawler.

We went to Sri Lanka for our honeymoon. I would always have recommended Sri Lanka highly but maybe not now with all the fighting and stampeding of political buildings, but it is a lovely place. The people are amazing and we loved the diversity of the country, including the tuk tuks and the exotic animals.

But the lasting impression was the people, they were just so hospitable and down to earth.

That second season with Benetton was when things started to click. The Pro14 had been expanded with the addition of two South African teams, the Bloemfontein-based Cheetahs and the Port Elizabeth-based Southern Kings.

We won away in the competition for the first time in four years against Edinburgh, where we had lost 45-10 almost 12 months before. This was pretty good considering we didn't check in to our hotel until 1am (Italian time) the night before the game due to the need for two flights, one of which was delayed. Now though, there was a shift in mentality that we could and should win away from home.

I started our opening Champions Cup game away to Bath in October 2017, when the goggles made their debut in the competition, and again a week later when we lost to the last kick of the game against a star-studded Toulon team.

The "Musketeer" friend group was created in the club, which was made up of captain Dean Budd, Seb Negri, Marty Banks and Rob Barbieri. I was probably a part-time member of this group, but good times were had.

And, again, with rugby players being rugby players, I wasn't immune from getting grief from the lads about my eye. On away trips we would usually get a flight to the games. We sat on the plane based on the alphabetical order of our last names so I always used to sit next to one guy in particular and he would use my lack of vision as part of a game. As he would sit to my left, he would quietly stuff bits of paper in the left side of my glasses while I was watching something on my Kindle or iPad. This paper would be quietly mounting up and it always took me ages to realise what was happening until I'd eventually turn to look at something and half a newspaper would fall onto the ground, surrounded by a big burst of laughter.

After playing in each of Benetton's first ten games of the season, starting eight of them, I was named in the Italian squad for the November series at home. This was my chance as Tommy Allan was injured but I felt my performances deserved this call up. We had a couple of pre-series camps in Treviso and Parma. This was really my first time working with Conor O'Shea and Mike Catt.

Conor was very approachable and had more of a director of rugby role within Italy. He'd had a very good playing career with London Irish and Ireland, and he is hugely respected in England for all the work he did at academy level and winning the Premiership with Harlequins in 2012, their first ever league title.

You could tell immediately he is a very intelligent person and put so much thought into his delivery of talks during the week of a camp or a game. While he left the majority of the coaching to the other coaches he was always on the pitch encouraging us. His family would fly over for the games and I remember his brother in particular being very kind to me with his words of encouragement. "What you have done is remarkable," he told me. "Just keep going, keep doing what you're doing."

I really enjoyed Mike as a coach and also had a really good relationship with him. He played professional rugby until he was nearly 40 and won a World Cup with England in 2003, so what was there not to learn from him? He brought a huge amount of positivity to the environment. Being on a team that was struggling in the Six Nations for a few years obviously was tough for players and, to counter this, he tried to make the guys think positively about rugby by introducing little games in team meetings just to put us in a good headspace.

Even though Mike brought a huge amount of energy to training, he had a good balance when explaining things in a very calm manner. He worked with me on my kicking, like the other kickers, but in particular on my 'blindspot'. He fully backed the players' decisions. He would devise some moves that were certainly different, like three-man line-outs or American football-style double switch plays which really got the mind going. I think if people were to analyse our attack or see the numbers when he was in charge, usually it was positive in comparison with other areas where we may have let ourselves down. When he was subsequently added to the Irish coaching ticket I always felt that he would have a very positive impact, especially with the experiences he had gained while coaching England and Italy.

We assembled as a squad on November 5th, a week before

our first game against Fiji in Catania, in Sicily. Along with the other Treviso-based lads, we flew from Venice to Catania. When we arrived at the hotel, we were greeted in the team room with the famous sweet treats of cannoli. They are Italian pastries made up of tube-shaped shells of fried pastry dough, filled with a sweet, creamy filling usually containing ricotta – a staple of Sicilian cuisine. It gave us plenty of energy for training anyway.

This was my first opportunity to meet some of the Italian lads that played abroad and greats like Leonardo Ghiraldini and Sergio Parisse. Usually Sunday was your travel day with a meeting in the evening, outlining how the week was shaping up. Monday was normally a touching base/preview day with Tuesday and Thursday being full-on if the game was on a Saturday.

The team announcement was on the Tuesday before our main pitch session. At the morning squad meeting before training the team was unveiled on a large screen and there was my name beside the number 22. The competitor in me wanted to be annoyed that I was only on the bench, but I was just so happy to be in the squad. Now I was closer than ever to fulfilling a dream which had looked so unlikely six years previously. I was full of confidence and couldn't wait for this game to arrive. Also, training was going well, and I was enjoying my rugby so much.

There were plenty of media interviews in the lead up to this game. I didn't mind doing media stuff, as long as it didn't interfere with my preparation. If people were, and are, genuinely interested in my story then I am more than happy to talk about it. It's a good platform for the goggles too, and helps me raise awareness about them for other people.

Over time, questions can become a bit repetitive but that really cannot be helped I suppose. However, I did always appreciate a journalist's efforts in approaching the subject from an obscure angle even if I would not quite give everything away, and for good reason. Journalists would often ask: "How has playing with one eye restricted your game?" and I would always dodge giving them a straight answer. There was no way I was going to go public and say: "By the way, I can't see my inside defender properly, playing at night affects my depth perception and kicking in the rain is a bit of a nightmare." I wouldn't be the first sportsman to refuse to give everything away to the media, and I won't be the last.

Cordelia, Mum, Dad, Philip and Emma all made the trip, their first to Sicily. Cordelia's journey was easier in comparison with the rest of the family. They only landed the night before the match as one of their Ryanair pilots did not show up, resulting in them missing a connecting flight. We met in the team hotel that evening just for a brief moment as they were shattered from travelling all day and I wanted to ensure I had the right amount of sleep.

The morning of the game arrived, and I prepped for it like I did for all my games, but what gave me confidence was that I knew I was ready for this moment. It wasn't just for me but for everyone who had helped me to this point. Before we took the bus to the stadium, the jerseys were handed out by Sergio to the guys who were earning their first cap. Jayden Hayward, Matteo Minozzi, Giovanni Licata and myself all received kind words and good luck from the great number eight.

Sergio is a living legend of the game and a player I idolised as a kid. He played so many high-quality games for his clubs in France as well as Italy. That week in Sicily was the first time I finally met him. He entered our team room and he commanded it, not only with size and stature, but also with his sheer presence. He could speak fluently in four languages; Italian, Spanish, French and English.

Although he was by now 34 he could still do so many things that were beyond the remit of most other players. He is certainly one of the most professional players I've come across in terms of preparation and recovery – normally the first to arrive and the last to leave. It must be very frustrating being on so many losing sides but he just kept coming back, always wanting to drive and raise standards.

When he presented me with my jersey before my first international he said: "I know a lot of people have the utmost respect for you and what you have done, and I certainly do too."

Coming from Sergio Parisse, how could you not be inspired by that? That blue jersey meant even more to me.

It's funny how perspectives change. As a child I would have worn my green Ireland jersey when running around the back garden envisaging a victory against the white jersey of England. Now I was wearing the blue Italian jersey against the white of Fiji and couldn't have been prouder.

Fiji had some world-class players in their line-up, like Leone Nakarawa and Levani Botia, so this was going to be a very tough game. They had beaten Italy the previous June in Suva. The atmosphere was building in the 25,000-seater Stadio Angelo Massimino football stadium. Both teams ran out from the tunnel to a massive reception which is great because rugby in Sicily wouldn't be as big as it is in Rome or northern Italy.

I have always loved anthems. Growing up in Whitechurch, during ad breaks in a TV programme we were watching, I would put a video of a game into the video player and watch the anthems until the programme was back on. The Meda Dau Doka, or God Bless Fiji anthem, was played and then it was our turn. I had known the words for years prior to this moment but Fratelli D'Italia started. I am tone deaf, but I belted it out with all my heart – I think making my teammate Dean Budd partially deaf in the process! But all I could see was my family in the grandstand with tears in their eyes while waving Italian flags.

The final pre-game act was the Cibi, the Fijians' war dance, and we were ready to go. The game was in the balance and on 60 minutes, I was given a nod from the Italian team manager that I was going on. We were leading 16-10 and, as I was putting on my goggles and scrum cap on all I thought was: 'Just do your fucking job and carry this result over the line.' The last 20 minutes played out well for us and I was able to kick my first ever international points with a penalty to seal the 19-10 win.

In the dressing-room afterwards an ex-Italian international, whose name I regret to say I cannot recall, said to me: "You're in a very elite group, winning your first cap and winning your first game on the same day!" I'll always remember those words.

The security was really tight after the game so it was a struggle to see my family. They gradually made their way down to the side of the pitch, where we asked a security guard to take a family photo. The stewards really didn't want my family to come onto the pitch and I was getting very annoyed because without them, I wouldn't have been on the pitch in the first place. Finally this tall, thin security guard relented and allowed everyone to nip through a gate onto the athletics track that surrounded the playing field. There were massive hugs between us all, a quick picture and just a feeling of pure pride and happiness.

Following that, I had to do a drugs' test post-game with Jayden Hayward and a couple of Fijian players. If you talk to any player about a post-game drugs' test they will tell you it can take two minutes or it can take two hours, depending on how quickly you can pee or the person in front of you pees. I didn't keep a note of the time, but it took absolutely ages.

It's a very surreal moment when you walk back into the changing room and it's completely empty and you're the only player there. Yet this time to myself was a nice time-out. The changing room had been cleaned up – everyone is into sweeping up the room nowadays – and it was just me and my bag. Still wearing my boots and playing kit, but no goggles or scrum cap, I sat down for a few moments and allowed myself a little time to reflect on the magnitude of this day.

I had a flashback of that day when I suffered my eye injury playing for UCD, seeing the trainee in the Eye and Ear Hospital, and being left on my own for 45 minutes in a room until they told me a specialist was coming in to see me.

I reflected on that day and on those 45 minutes on my own and thought: 'That's where you were then and look at where you are now. You're sitting in an Italian changing room, covered in a few scratches and bruises, and wearing an Italian jersey.'

I've rarely felt more content. It was one of the happiest moments of my life.

I showered and changed quickly, did a few media interviews and was pleasantly surprised that the bus was still there waiting for me. The atmosphere among the squad was buoyant. Victories didn't come along too often and this was a massive one. Fiji were ranked two places above us in the top ten in the world at the time.

Back in the team hotel I went up to my room and changed out of my tracksuit and into my suit, because we had the gala post-match dinner later, and quickly went back down to the reception area to my family. Cordelia, Philip, Emma, Mum and Dad were all there.

Andrew wasn't there because he couldn't get time off work but he was coming out for the last game of the November series against South Africa.

We hugged, took photos, reminisced about the journey to this point, and savoured the moment. Everything that we had all fought for as a family was for this day and it felt so, so satisfying. I wasn't just happy for myself but for my whole family. This monumental achievement was due to everyone's contribution. What I was particularly grateful for, and always will be, was that they all pulled together with their resources as best they could for me. So it would have been very selfish of me to have celebrated the moment just for myself. That night, those moments together, however brief, were a reward for everyone's efforts. I worked my butt off. I trained every day to learn again how to catch a ball, how to kick a ball, how to reprogram my brain with the goggles, and help lead the campaigns off the pitch, which was a tireless effort. I had to think more than an average rugby player in order to play with one eye and the goggles, but that day would not have been possible without each and every one of my family making that possible to achieve.

•••••

We just had huge pride as a family that night. They'd always been there, from early GAA days and my first Under-13 rugby matches but of course this one was hugely significant. This was brilliant for them too.

Emma would say to me: "God, our lives are not very exciting without you Ian. You make us travel to all these different places and make us explore different parts of the world and meet different people."

And that highlights the merits of the residency ruling. You see all of Bundee Aki's family all wearing green in Wellington when Ireland beat the All Blacks. There were my family wearing blue Italian jerseys in Sicily, as they would again in Florence, Padua, Chicago, Rome, Dublin and elsewhere in games to come.

Their Italian wouldn't be fantastic. They don't look particularly Italian. People would approach them and ask: "Why are you cheering for Italy?"

"Because my son plays for Italy."

All of that provides so much positive energy.

I don't think I could say it was a pinch-me-I-must-be-dreaming day or night, because I had set playing for Italy as a goal in 2014. I fully believed I could achieve that ambition. I was prepared for it. But looking back now, to have done so in three years was not bad.

My phone was inundated with text messages congratulating me before and after the game. Johnny Sexton and Joe Schmidt both did so as soon as the team was announced publicly. I had messages from people I hadn't heard from in years, from old school friends, from Cordelia's friends, ex-rugby teammates and coaches, from everywhere really.

On social media I received innumerable messages from

people who are visually impaired or from relatives of theirs, and others who just knew of my story. I'm not very active on my Twitter, Facebook or Instagram platforms, but whenever I looked that week they were cluttered, and I still receive those messages to this day.

But I definitely believe that week was all the sweeter because we actually won. If we'd lost it would have been a damp squib.

Not that we had much time together as a family that night. We didn't speak about the game in-depth. Philip and Dad love talking about the game, whether it's good or bad, afterwards. I generally try to forget about it until I review it. That's how I dealt with my post-match thoughts.

You couldn't help but go through moments or aspects of the game in your head and I'm sure, like virtually all players, I struggled to sleep on match nights. So if they asked: 'What happened there?' I tended to give them relatively short answers. I wouldn't go into too much depth until the review, which would invariably be fairly forensic anyway.

I'm also sure that if you ask most professional sports' people they'd feel the same. You spend the whole week, or even a period of weeks depending on the importance of the occasion, preparing physically and mentally for this one event. Then the one event happens and you generally experience either a massive emotional low or high depending on the result, usually with little in between these two extremes. I tried, although it's not easy, to stay somewhere in between; not become too carried away with myself if the day went well and be too hard on myself if it was a bad day. To achieve that, I tried to zone out rather than relive the game. I found that even more draining.

My family mingled with some of the Benetton players and coaches they knew. Kieran Crowley and his wife were there as well. Philip and Dad would have had no bother going up to Conor O'Shea or some of the Benetton players. Then they went out for a meal together in Catania.

I had been the last player on the team bus, but the first player down in the reception area, just to spend as much time as I could with my family until the team bus took us into Catania city centre for the post-match dinner.

The Italian post-match dinners are in museums, art galleries or swanky hotels. In other words, the settings are usually stunning. This was spectacular. We had an aperitivo and a meal with the Fijian team. As is the custom after internationals, the captains and the presidents of the federations or unions speak.

Jayden, Giovanni, Matteo and myself, along with Fiji's Semi Kunatani and Ropate Rinakama, were each individually presented with our first caps. Each time all the players in the room stood up and applauded.

One thing I'll never forget is the Fijian players then standing up and breaking into song. Apart from them you couldn't hear a pin drop. Everybody stopped talking. Seeing these massive Fijian rugby players sing what sounded like a soft hymn, or at any rate something so tranquil, after trying to beat the crap out of each other for 80 minutes was not something many of us in the room would ever have heard before. That probably prompted the biggest round of applause of the night.

Some guys decided to venture into the night. Some of us, including me, went back to the hotel but I did, I definitely did, have a couple of drinks. Probably not the wisest decision with two more games on the next two Saturdays but I'm normally quite bad for not savouring the moments.

I remembered Philip saying to me when this comeback started: "You've got to celebrate every milestone." This, he said, applied to everyone's life but with regard to my rugby journey this meant celebrating my first game in the Pro12, my first game in the Challenge Cup, my first game in the Champions Cup, my first time playing in England, all these ground-breaking achievements that no-one else had ever done.

And there wasn't going to be a much bigger milestone than winning your first international cap.

So that night, I could allow myself to let my hair down a little. I wasn't alone. This was Italy's first win since beating South Africa 12 months earlier so Sergio and the guys wanted to savour the moment too.

We had to undergo our medical check the following morning before the squad flew to Florence for our next game against Argentina. I had been to Florence a few times over the years as a tourist and also visited my friend Nick Civetta, who I played with in Viadana. He played there for a season at a club called

I Medicei. We also had training camps with Benetton close to Florence as a club sponsor was based there. They produced olive oil so we stayed in and amongst the olive groves. Dad, Emma and Philip had to fly home, but Mum came back and forth for each of the three matches.

For the game in Florence, Mum and Cordelia were joined by my mate Stew and his now wife Christina. Conditions were perfect for a game of rugby, but it was a slightly strange match. We were really in it for 65 minutes and then just seemed to collapse, which was the complete opposite of the week before. I came on for the last eight minutes and spent most of the time defending. We lost 31-15. Nicolas Sanchez, Argentina's out half, came up to me after the game and said: "You have inspired a lot of people." That was a nice touch.

A week later in Padova for our third and final game of the autumn series, there wasn't the same love from the South Africans. The Boks were in vengeful mood for the 20-18 defeat by Italy in Florence a year previously. We were smashed in one of the most physical games I have ever played in and it was made more difficult by the rain.

I came on for the last 25 minutes with the score 28-6 to them and we spent 20 minutes of that time in their half but we just could not break them down.

We made a break close to the line, I saw Handrè Pollard and thought I would go hard at him with a slight outside line. He absolutely smashed me. Needless to say I didn't try that again that day. When on form he is a very good out-half. They won 35-6.

Cordelia, Mum and Philip were all at this game, which was the first international match my brother Andrew and my in-laws attended. I managed to acquire them tickets in an area just outside the changing room where the players were coming and going. My in-laws had been to Ulster-Benetton games before, but I don't think they had ever seen human beings as big. Until that day they thought I was big, despite me assuring them otherwise, but thereafter they believed me.

For the 2018 Six Nations there was a three-way battle for the '10' jersey between Tommy Allan, Carlo Canna and myself. Although I was in the squad, I wasn't picked for any matchday squads which is a difficult place to be in because you end up not really playing for the national team or your club during that window.

I did play for Benetton in a win away to the Dragons in the first down week in the Six Nations, and then headed straight back to Rome to link up with the Italian squad. There was plenty of travel during that Six Nations for precious little game time and as Rome is quite a distance from Treviso I didn't see much of Cordelia or my family for those eight weeks.

The night before Italy were beaten at home by Scotland in their final Six Nations game, I was released to play for Benetton away to Cardiff. We lost 31-25. I spotted a half gap and took it. I thought I was away but was tackled from behind. When I fell, my knee hit the synthetic Cardiff Arms Park turf and I felt a sharp pain. Unfortunately, the hard surface did not help me. I continued the game in agony as Marty Banks had to go off injured and I was later told I had a chronic knee injury. I left Wales on a pair of crutches but thankfully I was only out for a few weeks.

After rehabbing the knee, I got myself back on the bench for our historic win over Leinster in the RDS which put a stop to their 36-match winning streak at home and in doing so we became the first Italian club side to win in Dublin. Unfortunately, I didn't get on the pitch as I had a recurrence of the knee injury I had sustained a few weeks earlier, bizarrely whilst warming up with the replacements during the game. Luckily enough, I wasn't needed but it did ultimately put an end to my season. However, it was still a very special result and showed how much this squad had grown.

Over the course of our 21 games in the Pro14 we recorded the highest number of wins by a Benetton team (11) since they first entered the Celtic League in 2010 and accumulated the club's highest points tally of 55. That would have been enough to qualify for the play-offs in Conference A, but not from Conference B, where we just missed out.

I also missed the summer tour to Japan and the start of the following season, and I still have some pain in my knee to this day. Players either love or hate those synthetic pitches.

I don't love them.

TWELVE

Missing Out

THE WEATHER could be so hot and humid for the pre-season games in Treviso that there was usually an influx of mosquitoes at Stadio Monigo. This had its issues, especially for me. In one particular match in August 2018, against Leicester, a mosquito flew into my goggles. So, while I was in the middle of orchestrating play, this thing was flapping around in my goggles. Thankfully, one of my teammates knocked on and during the pause in play I was able to take the goggles off briefly and quickly clean them. I've never been so grateful for one of my teammates knocking on. They have big mosquitoes in Treviso.

Recruitment had been effective over the previous two close seasons, and we had a good squad not only on but off the field as well.

Both the medical, and strength and conditioning staff had been developed much more. Previously we had two physios and two strength and conditioning coaches for the whole squad but now we had double that number.

One of our players, Nasi Manu, received the terrible news that he had testicular cancer so all of us, including staff members, shaved our heads in support of him. Thankfully he came through it and recovered, but events like that brought us closer together.

In previous years there would have been a massive turnover of players, but now we had a solid base with some clever signings who were not household names and came in under the radar, but were good for us. For example, the previous year Benetton signed Whetu Douglas, a back-rower, who had been starting for the Crusaders. Anyone who was starting for the Crusaders is obviously a very good player.

He only stayed for one season but there was still a really good balance of players going into the 2018-19 season, like Irne Herbst in the engine room, Monty Ioane on the wing and young up-and-coming Italian players like Michele Lamaro, who now captains Italy.

So we just needed a few subtle additions, and Marco Zanon, Dewaldt Duvenage, a scrum-half from the Stormers, and the backrower Toa Halafihi from Taranaki, all joined.

Marty Banks moved on and Antonio Rizzi, who I coached for two years at Under-16 level with Leonorso, also signed for us, so now we were going to be competing for the same position.

Antonio was 20 when he joined, and with Tommy Allan and

myself there, he knew he was at a stage of his career when he needed to learn and improve as much as he could. He was always very quick and coaching him as a kid you knew that he had all the skill set to be a really good player. He's been unfortunate to suffer a few injuries.

It never felt like we were intense rivals. In Udine I had been invited over to his house for family dinners when Antonio was 15. So while we were competing, I still felt that I was mentoring him. Whenever we were doing kicking sessions it still felt as if I was coaching him back in Udine with Leonorso, although his kicking had improved considerably.

I missed our first three games with my knee problem and made my return away to the Ospreys when replacing Antonio, who was making his full debut. In the dressing-room afterwards I took a photo of the two of us together. By his own admission he didn't have a great game so he was a little down, but it was a nice moment to share, albeit a slightly strange one as well.

I picked up a dead leg against the Southern Kings in just my third game back, which absolutely scuppered me. I was on crutches for a week and missed another four games. By the time I travelled with the Italian squad to Chicago for our first November game against Ireland in Soldier Field, it was my first game in five weeks, and I hadn't even played 80 minutes in total that season. I wasn't nearly as match sharp as I would have liked.

We travelled over a week before the game, taking special hydration gels and while the coaches flew economy class the players were in business class. After we touched down at O'Hare International Airport, the first thing to do was get rid of the jet lag in a short space of time. The training was overseen by Pete Atkinson, the strength and conditioning coach now with Wasps, whose attention to detail in everything we did began on the plane and on the first two days after flying there was walking and jogging but no sprinting. We trained on the back pitch of the Chicago Fire MLS football team.

There was plenty of press interest in me leading up to the game as this was my first time playing against my home nation. On the Thursday in our base for the week, the Palmer House Hilton Hotel, I did a telephone interview with Tuttosport, a Skype interview with CNN and another with an Irish newspaper journalist.

I did the CNN interview with my teammate Luca Morisi. Luca had to have emergency surgery to remove his spleen in 2013 after being on the receiving end of a tackle against Fiji. The American interviewers couldn't believe a guy "missing an eye" and another "missing a spleen" following rugby incidents would still want to play the game!

A few, slightly odd, memories stand out from that day, like seeing my old Irish Under-20 teammates Jack McGrath, Rhys Ruddock and John Cooney wearing green during the warm-up at the other end of the pitch.

It is becoming more common – due to the residency rule – for players to face each as rivals having previously grown up together as teammates, but back then it was still fairly rare. You try not to be too pally before the match – you can say hello after the game – but if I was practising my restarts on the halfway line, players you've known your whole career are sometimes only metres away so you would of course share the odd handshake or nod of the head. The really surreal part of that day was getting to the stadium and seeing all the green flags and jerseys and then seeing my family – as proudly Irish as they come – all wearing the blue of Italy!

I had lived with Rhys, while Jack and John were also in the academy with me, and I also played with John at UCD. Andrew Conway and Devin Toner were also playing for Ireland that day, and they had been Leinster teammates, and I knew Jordi Murphy and Luke McGrath from my Leinster academy days as well.

Like me, Big Dev was a replacement that day in Chicago, and he had been a teammate in all of my six senior games for Leinster. By the law of averages perhaps that's not surprising. He did play 280 games for Leinster. I suppose playing regularly for Benetton meant I came up against these guys on a regular basis, which made that part of the experience less unusual.

In the tunnel we were slightly ahead of Ireland but I just remember making eye contact with Josh van der Flier, and we gave each other a quick nod as if to say best of luck, before running out on the pitch. I was immediately struck by the amount of green in the stadium as well.

I didn't know how I was going to react hearing 'Ireland's Call' but I managed not to sing along before I blared out 'Fratelli D'Italia'. I actually tried not to use up all my energy in singing the anthems, so one anthem was enough.

I couldn't have been prouder that day to be pulling on the blue jersey of Italy but I was hugely disappointed with the result and how we played. They absolutely pummelled us in the second-half. I came on after an hour when the score was already 35-7. Jordan Larmour was on fire that day and scored a hat-trick.

Our game was the second of a triple header in Soldier Field, and was followed by a game between the USA Eagles and the New Zealand Maori, with my American friend Nick Civetta playing for America.

I caught up with him a couple of times during that week and then met with John Cooney afterwards when he came into the changing room and we swapped jerseys. I spoke with Rhys and Joe briefly too but only after the game as Ireland had landed in the middle of the week and were on a tighter schedule.

Ronan O'Gara was at the game, watching as a fan and no doubt picking up tips for his coaching career. We had a quick chat because after my debut against Fiji, Ronan had congratulated me on TV for showing the courage and tenacity to get to international level, which was very high praise indeed.

I had remembered that so I wanted to introduce myself in person. However, I'm not entirely convinced he even recognised who I was without my goggles and scrum cap on! Ronan had one of the finest ever Ireland careers so I let him away with it. By the way, we have worked on TV together since and I still don't call him 'Rog' – that is a name reserved for those closer to him than I am.

I had been a non-playing reserve, or 24th man, the previous February when Italy played Ireland at the Aviva Stadium and while playing against Ireland in Chicago was a milestone I knew, or certainly hoped, that there might be more meaningful games, such as in the Six Nations.

While Dad was watching back at home, Mum, Emma, Philip and Cordelia were all in Chicago. They had been on the same flight from Dublin with some of the Irish players' parents, although few were from my time in the Irish Under-20s or Leinster so they didn't know many of them. My family came over for the weekend and I didn't see much of them until after the game when they came to the hotel.

My family were really excited to see Nigel Owens, for some reason! They duly met him and took a photo with him. The Italian squad were having dinner in Michael Jordan's Steak House and I politely asked our team manager if my family could join us for dinner. They very kindly allowed that, so the four of them ate with the team.

The next day I flew back to Rome with the squad and then travelled on to Treviso. The squad had been somewhat split, and in the pre-November camp Conor had said he was going to use

Tommy Allan and Carlo Cana Canna in their remaining games against Georgia, Australia and New Zealand.

•••••

As I hadn't had much game time, I needed some matches under my belt to push for a spot in the Six Nations.

I had a busy time of it then too, starting away against both South African teams, both Challenge Cup games against Harlequins, with a dramatic win in the first, and then Zebre. At the end of January, I captained Benetton against Ulster in Belfast.

In a previous Zebre game in Belfast both my nephews, Nathan and Matthew, had been mascots and were led onto the pitch by ex-Italian captain Marco Bortolami. For this one I led out the team with my nephew Cameron and my niece, Isobel, as mascots, which is one of the favourite memories of my career. It had to be done then because Cameron is three inches taller than me now. Not a good look if the ball boy is taller than you! A picture of this happens to be the main poster shot of the Netflix 'Look Beyond' documentary. So, all in all, four McKinleys have been mascots at the Kingspan.

Ulster were awarded a last-minute penalty try to make it a 17-all draw, and after an additional 48 seconds that should not have been added on.

That denied Benetton a sixth win in a row in both competitions. We did enough to win. It was not a happy away dressing-room. But that also showed the shift in our mentality. A week later though I fulfilled another childhood dream when I made my Six Nations debut in our opening game against Scotland in Murrayfield. In fact, I played in four of our five games.

The Six Nations certainly is a different animal from November matches. The intensity of being in camp and everything else is ramped up. I had a fairly good idea of this from being an unused member of the squad a year previously. But until you play the games you don't appreciate the speed, physicality and decision-making has to be spot on.

It was another milestone for the goggles, but me and they were going to be tested like never before. It was tough, more demanding mentally and errors were punished more ruthlessly. As I'm sure most players will confirm, you've a split second less to make a decision. You have less time to adapt.

I had limited game time and certainly less than I would have liked. Every player wants to play 80 minutes of every game, but I also appreciated this was something of a learning curve as well, especially in how the goggles could adapt to that level. I was still figuring that out.

In the Pro14 you became used to playing in Cardiff Arms Park or the Sportsground. You knew what the lights were like. Playing in the Stadio Olimpico, Twickenham and the Aviva Stadium was all very new and very different – as well as being at a faster pace and more physical – and it challenged me and the goggles. They were bigger stages, with bigger crowds too, but that's the part you grow up loving and wanting to experience. Difficulties arose though if the goggles were affected by a little water or mud, as everything went so much quicker. And any weakness was exploited.

If I struggled with a pass it was amplified that bit more. It just became that bit more obvious. It was the micro details. If I looked back at a game on video I might see a little gap which I missed at the time. If I couldn't see my inside defender, in a Pro14 game I might be able to scrag the ball carrier or my inside defender might have tackled him, or I might even have tackled him with a dominant tackle. But if it's not a dominant tackle at international level it's either a line break for the opposition or the carrier is able to offload and you're retreating five, ten or 20 metres.

All of this frustrated me deeply because previously I knew I would have seen that through the side of my eye.

We were competitive against both Scotland in Murrayfield and Wales in Rome, but still lost both games 33-20 and 26-15, before we had Ireland at home in round three at the Stadio Olimpico.

Personally, I would love to have played in Italy's original ground in Rome, the Stadio Flaminio. I think a smaller capacity and having the crowd so close would make it a more atmospheric ground and more difficult for away teams.

There are some features on the long driveway to the Stadio

Olimpico which are amazing – a gladiatorial ring with a rugby pitch, like a mini colosseum, and the Foro Italico tennis courts where the Italian Open is held every year.

We always changed in the Lazio changing rooms and when we had our captain's run the day before our game each seat had the names of the Lazio players who had played there a few days beforehand.

However, as usual, the stadium wasn't packed out, about 20,000 short of a full house, which is tough. You'd see at least 50 per cent away support and the fans are further away from the pitch, which definitely made it feel less of a home game. But we also knew that was because we weren't getting results.

I was annoyed by that game because I missed a late penalty to earn us a losing bonus point. Not an easy kick, from near the touchline, but if you are brought on with five minutes remaining that is your job. You look at Morné Steyn. Whenever he is brought on late in a match, he always nails those clutch kicks. I know I was comparatively new to international rugby but those were the things that would irritate me. It mightn't seem much but earning a losing point against Ireland would have been something tangible.

After the post-match meal Rob Kearney, Peter O'Mahony, my Irish Under-20s captain, and Johnny Sexton were sitting together, and I went over to them for a chat.

It was a very quick chat about our families and life in general – nothing too major – but I was still a little sheepish after the game because we lost. I didn't want to lose. We didn't want to lose.

Of course, we'd share a laugh and a beer together after the match, but this was now my second defeat by Ireland. The first one was by a really big margin and while this was only by ten points, we had a chance to potentially take something from this game. So, it hurt, which makes it harder to approach and talk to people when you know you haven't played to your best. Whether that's me being too self-critical I don't know but that was the way my mind worked.

Our one heavy defeat (57-14) was by England in Twickenham when I had my longest stint on the pitch, but at full-back and outside centre because of two early injuries in the game. We lost Michele Campagnano and Tommy Castello, his replacement at centre, and Tommy ended up having to retire at the age of 30 because of the leg injury he sustained that day. Tommy never played again. We also lost our other starting centre, Luca Morisi, in the second-half.

So, Jayden Hayward and I had to play together in midfield. Combined, I think we weighed less than 180kg and we were going up against Ben Te'o and Manu Tuilagi, who probably weighed a bit north of 220kg in total.

To cap that, even the rain trickled down, which is not easy when playing with the goggles at Twickenham. However tough it was playing Harlequins just down the road in Europe the previous December, which was obviously a good standard, or even making up the step up to November internationals, the difficulty increases tenfold when it's England, Twickenham, they're rampant, the rain is affecting your vision and you've got guys like Billy Vunipola and Tuilagi coming at you. I can think of better days in my career.

We very nearly beat France, and had chances to do so, on the last day at the Stadio Olimpico, but Damian Penaud knocked the ball from the hands of Marco Zanon when he was about to put us ahead late on and then scored a try himself.

Antoine Dupont scored the first try and although Romain Ntamack didn't have a great match, he nailed all his kicks and created that Penaud try with a brilliant offload.

The final table shows we didn't win any games, so you can't say it was a good tournament. Yes, four of them were within 13 points, which was better than previous years but, ultimately, we still lost all five matches, and you can't dress that up any other way.

I wasn't given much game time, especially at out-half, and one of the objectives before the tournament was to earn a start. I don't like coming off the bench, even at club level. Any out-half will tell you they like to be starting and so be able to control the game from the kick-off.

Unlike in Ireland, where guys could go home for a night from Carton House, when you're in camp in Rome you stay there as the train journey to Treviso takes over four hours.

But I did make that return journey for two Treviso games

during the Six Nations as, like the year before, it was another hectic time. I played the full 80 in Benetton's 25-19 win over Scarlets at home, kicking 10 points, on the weekend before the Ireland game, and the same a week after it when we beat Edinburgh at home. As they were our nearest challengers in Conference B, they were very important wins. So this was a really exciting time for Benetton as we were fighting for a place in the play-offs.

I would captain the side in three games that season. We won four out of six in Europe, just missing out on the Challenge Cup knockout stages, and again won 11 games in the Pro14 and drew two more to finish on 57 points, a further improvement on the previous campaign.

We finished third in our conference, above the Scarlets and Edinburgh, to become the first Italian side ever to reach the play-offs. To go from last place to the play-offs in the space of three years was an amazing achievement.

But when I started in the Sportsground against Connacht a week later I suffered another knee injury after half an hour. That ruled me out of the run-in against Leinster, when we drew 27-all at the RDS, Munster and Zebre, and in the quarter-finals, when we lost narrowly and unluckily (15-13) against Munster at Thomond Park.

That wasn't ideal with the World Cup in Japan on the horizon the following September but after a four-week break I was ready for the start of Italy's pre-season in early June. We mixed up our training camps. Our international contingent in Benetton trained in Treviso and likewise the Zebre contingent in Parma, and then those playing outside did their own thing with their clubs before we came together en bloc, either in the Dolomites or in Treviso. When we trained together, we were based mainly up in the cooler temperatures nestled in the Dolomites.

It was pretty gruelling but I was probably in the best shape of my career, and the same for all the other lads. The great Wayne Smith was brought in to a few of our training camps to give us a helping hand. People talk about him in such reverential terms and I could see why. He is just brilliant. He is very calm and clear in what he wants. We didn't have him for a huge amount of time in the grand scheme of things, but you could tell that he is one of the very best coaches in the world.

Eddie Jones also brought the English squad to Treviso as he reckoned the summer weather and humidity levels in the Veneto region of northern Italy were similar to Japan. So we trained against them with both Treviso and the Italian squad.

Even though we were training against England, we were in different camps and we very much did our own thing. When you train against another country, even though it is not a game, you do try and find another level, and we were as competitive as could be. There were no blow-out scraps like England had against Georgia before the 2019 World Cup but both sets of players gave it everything.

You could see that Eddie was the general – he was watching

everything that was going on – and he left the coaches to their individual roles but he was always overlooking everything. We briefly shook hands but we didn't have long conversations. Conor and Mike probably had more in-depth talks following their own time in England.

England came over with massive lorry loads, be it their kit, equipment, protein shakes or whatever. They even had their families flown over to have a holiday and support the squad, booking out an entire hotel. Their expenditure and preparation were on a different level.

I knew I didn't have a good Six Nations. When I don't embrace the occasion, I become too tense and then don't perform. I wanted to do so well that it actually translated into negative performances. Even when you're only given six minutes and you have a kick to win or draw the game, or in my case salvage a bonus point, you still have to do your role, which I didn't do.

So training was going to be important to show the coaches that you deserved to be picked but I didn't have much luck at the camps because at each one I was sick. Vomiting, diarrhoea – you name it, I seemed to get it all for some reason, and as with any 24 hour-bug it takes you a day or two to fully recover. Also, in one particular training session I even had my two front teeth knocked out during a defensive exercise which meant I had to wear a brace for a while.

Our first World Cup warm-up game and also our last before Conor O'Shea finalised the 31-man squad for the World Cup, was against Ireland at the Aviva Stadium on August 10th 2019. Conor informed me in advance that I would be playing the second-half and at half-time I was one of three players brought on for Italy.

In my back garden I had imagined listening to 'Amhrán na bhFiann' before playing for Ireland at the old Lansdowne Road. I had been there as 24th man in the 2018 Six Nations but this was the first time I had lined up on the pitch listening to the Irish national anthem and 'Ireland's Call'.

Random people had asked me beforehand: "What are you going to do? Are you going to sing the Irish national anthem?"

I suppose you don't really know until you're in that moment, but I was pretty certain I wasn't going to do so, that I would blare out 'Fratelli D'Italia' as I had done in Chicago and Rome. And, unfortunately for whoever was in earshot, I did.

As a kid I had dreamed of playing at Lansdowne Road for Ireland. When I was permitted to play with the goggles, I then dreamed of playing there for Italy. I didn't dream though of a kick of mine being blocked down for an Irish try. So, it was a bit of a nightmare and not one I want to remember. That was one of my last acts as an international rugby player and will forever live with me.

I knew that my chances of going to the World Cup were slim as I hadn't started that game and my performance wasn't good enough. I was in a fairly foul mood after the game and couldn't wait to return to Italy, just to bury my head in the sand. I know these things happen but it seemed like all my little mistakes were all at international level, and were all magnified by what happened next, whereas they weren't happening at club level. But, of course, that's because I was playing at a more elevated level, and with the pressure that accompanies Test rugby.

Like a stress test, I was also put under more pressure with the goggles. I was just very frustrated.

We travelled back the morning after the game to Rome. From there we had a four-hour bus journey from the airport to our next venue, San Benedetto del Tronto on the coast of the Adriatic Sea, where we were playing Russia the following Saturday. I remember it was four hours because the air conditioning in the bus wasn't working and we were driving in near 40 degree heat.

Although the 31-man squad for the World Cup was not submitted until the day after the Russian game, we had one more session together as a squad on the Monday before the dreaded cuts were made. We were told that evening.

We all knew that Conor would be approaching those players who were missing the cut one-on-one and so have a chat with each player, and you could tell what was happening. As I was walking from the team room back to my room he saw me and asked for a chat. We went to an outdoor area of our hotel and I knew, one hundred per cent, what was coming. Carlo had started against Ireland at '10' and I knew that Tommy Allan would be starting the Russian game. What's more, my performance hadn't helped my chances.

Conor informed me I hadn't made the cut and said: "This was a very, very difficult decision and you made it more difficult." Well, that at least was what I said I'd do when I first met him that day in La Ghirada after becoming eligible. He thanked me for all the hard work I had put in and said to stay fit in case anything happened. That was it really. There was no flipping the table or anything like that. I can't remember how long we spoke for, or whether he gave any reasons, but it was very amicable.

Yet in those minutes I felt so low. You dream of something from the age of five and then, having come so close, that dream is dashed forever.

It would have been a perfect way to close a ten-year cycle from representing Ireland at a Junior World Championship in Japan in 2009, when I captained the team in one of the games, to then representing Italy at the World Cup in Japan in 2019, all the more so given the madness in between. Unfortunately, it was not to be. That's the nature of the business. But it was very upsetting. I'm sure Big Dev wouldn't have been too happy when he had his conversation with Joe that same week.

Most coaches went with a 17-14 split and brought three out-halves to the World Cup. Conor opted for an 18-13 split and two out-halves. But that is just clutching at straws. Ultimately playing with the goggles in international rugby is just another level, not that I am making excuses.

I had to look at myself first and I know I didn't give the best account of myself on the pitch in the Six Nations or the warm-up game against Ireland. I felt a little angry and, in some ways, let down, but that was entirely with myself. Not anyone else.

For any coach who picked me since I acquired the goggles I can appreciate the leap of faith they took as well. Even though I never wanted to make goggles an issue, or the eye an issue, I know that they had to come into some consideration. You would hope your stats would alleviate those issues, but I appreciate coaches have to make a judgement call.

I am very much of the opinion that you make your own luck, and if you perform well enough, I would have gone to the World Cup. As I've said, one of my regrets was that I didn't master my kicking with one eye. Another regret, definitely, was not embracing my time at international level and making that step up to Test rugby and Six Nations rugby with the goggles. Although if that was a step up each time, I can only imagine what a World Cup would have been like.

So back to Treviso it was for the lads that were based there, Marco Zanon, Marco Lazzaroni, Angelo Esposito and myself. There wasn't any transport booked for us who didn't make it, so we basically rented two cars between the four of us and drove five hours to Treviso.

I needed a break and took ten days off. Training had been so intense. You can fill your head with rugby, and I wasn't feeling well physically. But like many people when you're working flat out at something for about two and a half months and then suddenly stop, your body gives up on you or goes into shock or something. Cordelia and I went to Amsterdam for a couple of nights and then home to Ireland for a few days. I was shattered. One night, and day, I slept solidly for about 20 hours in Cordelia's house. She said I needed to see a doctor, and I was diagnosed with shingles, which fairly floored me. Shingles is related to stress and your body being run down, which shows how athletes put themselves through the mill.

Then it was back to Treviso and Benetton, and watching the World Cup from home, including the Italian and Irish games. A tough watch in many ways.

So that was that.

My last game of international rugby had been at the Aviva. I suppose in some ways that was fitting.

—

THIRTEEN

Arrivederci, Italia

AFTER MISSING out on the World Cup and returning to Benetton, I never really had a look-in again. It was just a different atmosphere. I went back to holding a tackle bag for the week. Out of the 52 players in our squad, I was now very much number 52. I had almost become invisible.

To underline the point, one time we had a training session against an Eccellenza side and because there were so many players, we ended up using three pitches. I was kept on the far pitch with the younger kids and never called over to the main pitch during the rotation of players. The signals were not exactly positive.

This was certainly the total opposite of my Leinster academy days when Joe used to shout and roar at me, always trying to improve players. But in the final months at Benetton if I made a mistake in training it wasn't even picked up. It was just ignored. Previously it had always been about driving up standards. It was a complete flip. I was given the cold shoulder.

During the World Cup I was on the bench for the first three games of the Pro14 at home to Leinster, and away to Connacht and the Ospreys. But I only came on at out-half against Connacht. In the others I was at full-back. Ian Keatley had been signed and started all those matches, and once Tommy Allan came back from the World Cup, he was first-choice.

But after the World Cup, I was told that I wouldn't be picked again for two months.

I was then on the bench for our third round Champions Cup game away to Lyon. I came on early in the second-half, when we were 20-0 behind and, although we lost 28-0, I had a decent game. Certainly, some of the guys told me I had helped steer a sinking shop, because it could have been much worse.

I thought I would be involved in the squad again the following week but Keats started and Antonio was named on the bench. He'd made his only start of the season in the first Lyon game and would move on to Zebre at the end of the season after Paolo Garbisi joined.

There was no communication as to why until I confronted Kieran Crowley. This is the harsh side of professional sport, but I don't like it when I am not told things straight. I can deal with it one way or the other.

So, I had a fairly frank conversation with Kieran that week to see what was up. I said, bluntly: "Why the sudden change at the club? What's going on here?" And I was told in reply that they were focussing on younger players but given Keats was 32 at the start of that season and I was 29, that didn't really sit right with me. I had only turned 30 three days before playing against Lyon.

I've absolutely nothing against Keats. He's a lovely lad and a fantastic player. His numbers speak for themselves. But that reason didn't stack up. Whether there was another reason I don't know but that's what I was told, which was frustrating. I don't mind being told good news or bad news, but I'd rather it is straight and gives me something to work on.

Kieran is a very quiet man by nature. I do have the utmost respect for him as a player and a coach, and what he has achieved in the game. However, I was disappointed by the lack of transparency in that meeting and how it ended. I fully understand that rugby is ruthless and both clubs and coaches have to make decisions, but I'm big enough to take the bad news as well as the good. Instead, there was a lack of communication from the coaches.

After 67 games over a three-and-a-half-year period, captaining the side and being part of the various leadership groups since I arrived, my time at Benetton was done, sadly.

It was a very bitter pill to swallow because I was loving my rugby.

Of course, I had to cope with the disappointment of missing

out on World Cup selection. My emotions might have been more ramped up because I put so much of my energies into trying to make that Italian squad for the biggest event in world rugby, which only comes every four years. I knew it had been a once-in-a-lifetime opportunity for me.

But the total change in attitude rocked me.

I'd gone from competing for the Italian out-half spot, as well as occasional captain at Benetton and member of the leadership group, which had been decided by coaches and fellow players, and had been heavily involved over the previous three seasons, to fourth choice at the club and frozen out. It just didn't make sense.

My contract was up at the end of the season although I did play in two more games off the bench, away to Cardiff in February and the Dragons on March 6th. I came on for the last ten minutes and we won 37-25 with a bonus point.

The miracle was that the match even took place. It had been rescheduled after the original fixture had been called off due to bad weather three weeks' beforehand and by that first weekend of March 2020, the Covid-19 pandemic had begun to hit Italy especially.

February had seen the first positive cases and deaths in Italy due to the virus before anywhere else. The Ireland-Italy Six Nations game that weekend in Dublin, along with the women's and Under-20s matches, had been postponed a week previously.

Ours was a Friday game and we rocked up to the bus at the

training facility the previous morning. Our sporting director, Antonio Pavanello, had his phone to his ear trying to confirm whether or not we were taking the bus to the airport and flying to Bristol before taking another bus to Newport. Eleven towns in northern Italy were already in lockdown and we definitely did not want the worst-case scenario of being stranded in Bristol or Newport.

The game was eventually given the green light by the Pro14 after we had given assurances that no-one in our party had been in contact with anyone who had tested positive for the coronavirus.

We made our trip over through Marco Polo airport in Venice where the only people we encountered were ourselves and the airport staff.

We stayed in the Holiday Inn, where we normally stayed, and played the game in front of a crowd.

So, as events transpired, I started my club career with Leinster against the Dragons at Rodney Parade in Newport and finished it at the same ground almost 11 years later.

It was only on the bus back to our hotel in Bristol airport that guys were receiving messages saying that things were closing down. After the red eye flight back to Treviso the next morning, the club told us we had the week off pending further developments and some of the foreign players had to decide whether to go home, so as to avoid being in lockdown in Italy, or stay put.

Some did fly back to their families, while some of the other guys said to me: "Would you consider going home?"

"Sure, I am home," I always said. "This is where we live."

We had no real thought of going back to Ireland at that stage. We were just going to ride it out and see where it went. Events unfolded quickly.

Cordelia and I went for a meal on Sunday, March 8th, less than 48 hours after playing the Dragons, with my friend Dean Budd and his partner Amelia in a town about 30 or 40 minutes away from Treviso. Messages kept cropping up on our phones, one of which confirmed that Italian Prime Minister Giuseppe Conte had announced that 14 provinces in Lombardy and Veneto were being placed under quarantine, including Treviso, after the death toll passed 230. He described the coronavirus as the biggest threat to Italy since the Second World War.

"Wow, this is crazy," we said.

The following day, March 9th, all of Italy was placed under regional lockdown, and, inevitably, the Pro14 along with the whole of sport was suspended indefinitely by the end of that week, Friday March 13th.

The club told us that, if we wanted to, we could grab some gym equipment from La Ghirada. Slots had to be arranged in advance as we could go to the club two at a time. I drove to the club and took a few dumbbells, kettle bells, plates and a bar, and stored them in my garage.

Our movements were restricted from that first week. We

were only allowed to be in transit in case of an emergency and if we needed to go to work, we required completed forms with the necessary information of our employer.

Fortunately for the days and months ahead, in 2017 we added a dog to the family. We acquired her from a rescue shelter. She's a mix of an Italian greyhound and a whippet. She's teeny tiny, about seven kilos. She's as fast as lightning, just zips around the place. For some reason we called her Mela, which is apple in Italian. Don't ask me why.

Even when the province was initially closed, we went out for a little walk, which was allowed before Italy went into full lockdown. There was no traffic. I have videos of one of the streets beside us, which is one of the busiest roads in Treviso, and there just wasn't a soul. If you've watched an apocalyptic film, it was exactly the same.

Cordelia and I isolated ourselves in our apartment and watched the horror that was unfolding across Italy and then globally.

It was a very scary time to be living in Italy.

One of the memories, honestly, that sticks out is simply hearing nothing, just dead silence, punctuated every five or ten minutes by the sound of ambulance sirens. Normally you would hear planes and car horns, which are aplenty in Italy, but it was just deathly silence interrupted by ambulances.

In the lead-up to the Dragons game I had received a call from The Ryan Tubridy Show in RTÉ. Italy was the epicentre of the Covid-19 pandemic in Europe and at least a month ahead of Ireland and the UK in the grim coronavirus curve. There was always acute interest back in Ireland regarding developments in Italy; in numbers, the Government's response, lockdown measures and health forecasts. They were keen to know the details of daily life, and how the Italians were reacting.

I did a couple of interviews with Irish newspapers in the ensuing weeks as well and Cordelia also wrote several diaries for the Belfast Telegraph to give readers an insight into lockdown life in Italy and, by extension, what might be coming the way of Ireland.

In Cordelia's diary for the Belfast Telegraph on Wednesday 11th March 11th, she wrote: 'Later that evening, the Italian President held another press conference to inform the nation that we were currently in the midst of a lockdown and from now on, all non-essential work was to be closed except pharmacies, supermarkets and tabaccherie (newsagents). As well as not driving anywhere unnecessarily, we can no longer leave the house on foot unless we have an emergency or need to get groceries and if a Polizia stops you and you haven't an adequate reason to be out of the house, they can fine you €200. Fortunately for us, walking a dog falls under a "necessity" so we are able to take her out the usual couple of times a day. I think this will prove to be essential for our sanity in this period.'

On Friday 13th March 2020 – Day 6 – she wrote: 'This morning we walked Mela and popped in to see one of Ian's teammates and his family from their front garden to check in on them and talk to someone different! They told us that they are going home indefinitely as they don't know when things will get better and they can't work anyway.

'They have rented an apartment and plan to self-quarantine the first two weeks they are home to ensure they don't spread the virus in case they unknowingly have it. I will be sad to see them go as we'll miss the contact with friends who are within walking distance. They gave us a big box of all their perishable goods so they aren't wasted while they are away.

'I must say that I am jealous that they are going home and conflicted about our situation. I would much rather be at Ballyscullion where we have the luxury of space to move around and family to spend time with. However, the last thing either of us want to do is unwittingly carry the virus home and make our friends, family and strangers sick. We also don't want to leave behind our dog, not knowing when we will see her again.'

On Saturday 14th March 2020 - Day 7, she wrote: 'I woke up feeling quite anxious this morning, I spent far too much time yesterday online and I think all the panic has got to me slightly. It's also the third day of lockdown and hearing that other players and their families have gone home makes me feel a bit homesick. We no longer have the option of going home even if we wanted to as EasyJet and Ryanair have cancelled all flights between Ireland and Italy until mid-April at least. Now and again, I feel an overwhelming sense of claustrophobia.

'A 45-minute dog walk makes us feel better as well as doing some YouTube yoga videos and a fitness programme that the team sent over to Ian to keep them in relatively good condition while they are housebound.

'At around 16:30, we hear some music and go out on our balcony to listen to someone playing their clarinet. Unfortunately, it started raining almost immediately so we didn't get a chance to catch it on camera or appreciate for more than a minute. They must have been inspired by all of the cheering videos circling on social media of Italians playing their instruments on their balconies and having their neighbours join in. These videos put a smile on everyone's faces in an increasingly fraught period, as we learned today that in 24 hours 250 Italians died, the most in one day since the crisis began."

The news just kept getting worse and by March 21st, Italy's death toll had reached 5,400 and had overtaken China. There were particularly grim reports coming from Lombardy, with horrific shots of army trucks taking dead bodies to mass grave sites. Gradually, we tried not to read too much of the news or listen to it because otherwise it could put us into a deep state of depression.

So, we usually set our alarm for 8.30am. We just thought this was a happy medium between the previous normality and maintaining some form of regularity or discipline to our daily life in the new abnormal. I would look at the news in the morning and in the evening before going to bed just to keep tabs on things. Anything in between, we just didn't look at it. Maintaining a structure in our day was just so important. Doing some exercise could take you up to lunch time. Taking Mela for a walk or doing a shop could be the main event of the afternoon, and then do something after dinner. We tried to break it up into three different blocks.

In her diary of Wednesday 25th March 2020 – Day 18 – Cordelia wrote: 'Since my last post, we watched the death rate hit 790 last Saturday, then drop to 670 on Sunday and finally 602 on Monday before it spiked again to 743. We were filled with hope that the deaths were slowly falling and that there was light at the end of the tunnel. Even though the death rate has risen again, the lockdown is finally having the desired effect, the number of newly infected has slowed and that's the figure we should all be watching closely.

'Our isolation period effectively finishes on Friday 3rd of April but I wouldn't be surprised if this is extended for at least another week. The government needs to keep us shut away until there are no more new confirmed cases, otherwise the cycle starts again.

'On reflection, we are glad we made the decision not to go home when the quarantine commenced two weeks ago as we would have gone from one lockdown to another. This has happened to a number of Ian's colleagues who went home, they now have to live through an extended lockdown period. At least they are with their families, an unexpected bonus I'm sure!'

I suppose if you weren't in Italy it could have seemed worse from abroad, almost like parents watching a game in which their children are playing. It would have been tough for my family and Cordelia's, especially as her parents had many weddings booked for Ballyscullion Park, but we did speak regularly.

I would normally have spoken to my family once a week but during the lockdown I would have spoken with them every day, just to keep them abreast of everything. I'm sure they were more worried about us than they let on, and it was also intriguing that we were a month or five weeks ahead in Italy in the trajectory of the virus.

Yet the main thing was that we, and our families, were healthy. Others went through a lot worse situations, be it a family death or crumbling business. We were very fortunate to be in the situation we were in so we got on with it. It was a small sacrifice in the greater scheme of things if you're told to stay in the comfort of your home to ride this out.

I started reading much more, and cooked. Shopping was restricted to one person, and even with long queuing as part of the one-in, one-out system being enforced by supermarkets and butchers, this was a highlight of the week. Flour was the only foodstuff which was occasionally in short supply, because people were baking and making pasta from home like never before. I have a pasta making machine which Cordelia gave me for my birthday and I made a large variety of different pastas.

I absolutely love cooking and when you go to Italy, and there's a lockdown, you simply have no choice because the quality of food everywhere is just outstanding. I did an interview with the Pro14 website and I think the title was: 'I've learned how to make pasta – Ian McKinley in lockdown.' But that did sum it up.

My garage was actually too small even for my Polo. Their garages are built for miniature minis or Fiat 500s from the '50s and '60s whenever these luxury apartments were built!

We were relatively lucky to have an area around the apartment block for parking our cars, not with any green area, but enough to walk around a little bit or to run around my apartment block, which took about 20 seconds. I tried to come up with variations, but it was very difficult. As well as the small amount of equipment I had from the club, you use your body as the gym more than anything.

One of our neighbours made a timetable for people to use this area which was quickly removed by someone. The average age of the people in our block was probably on the older side, so I was the main one doing exercises. As the heat increased I trained from about 10am to midday, and that was me done for the day.

I trained every morning and we had constant meetings among the leadership group, of which I was still a part even though it didn't feel like it. We provided updates on what we were all doing and were continually informed about the extended restrictions regarding group training, as one week became two which became three and so on.

There were also ongoing discussions about players being paid given there were no matches taking place, which was worrying, but unlike many others we were still fortunate to be in a job. It must have been a pretty stressful time for Antonio Pavanello and the club hierarchy as well. But we were the relatively fortunate ones, particularly in Italy.

The first lockdown lasted over two months before, on May 16th, the Government announced they were easing restrictions, with social distancing, in what the Prime Minister admitted was "a calculated risk".

In late May/early June, travel to and from Italy, and between provinces, was restored, while shops and restaurants were reopened, with social distancing.

I knew my contract was not going to be renewed and that my time with Benetton was done. I put a feeder out there to see which clubs might be interested but my journey as a player at that level in Italy appeared to be over. Nobody was interested in my services.

I did receive some interest from outside Italy but none seemed to fit, not least as they were in places where it rained a heck of a lot more and the frustration I had with rain played into my decision.

I was close to signing as a full-time coach with a club near Treviso but unfortunately that fell through. Cordelia had also become pregnant and there was also the distinct possibility of another Covid-19 wave and further lockdowns. We asked ourselves did we necessarily want that for both sets of families? So, we made the decision to come back to Ireland and live closer to Cords' family in Bellaghy, which is in Northern Ireland.

There were players who had been in Treviso much longer than me who weren't afforded a send-off, simply because it wasn't possible. When we started back training in late May we were divided into three groups based on our living conditions; players who lived in an apartment without an area in which to run, those who had a garden and those who had been living abroad.

We initially trained without a ball. It was literally just running, and we had to keep ten metres apart. We weren't allowed to touch anything. There were strict guidelines on time keeping, i.e. not showing up early for your hour on the pitch and not staying a minute longer, which was very different as players like to arrive early and afterwards stay on to do extras.

Individual rugby balls were introduced for skill work and gym was even more strict. Each player had a station to themselves for a block of 45 minutes or an hour within a small group, at the end of which we had to wipe down everything religiously and depart through a different exit before the arrival of the next group, which would be half an hour later.

Training gradually increased to a reduced pre-season with contact work in June. Although I might have given a misleading impression, I truly don't drink much at all, but for the last session involving myself and others whose contract expired on

July 1st, we brought in a case of beer and a few of us sat down on the pitch and toasted those who were leaving.

I remember having a beer and a chat in a group with Seb Negri, Tommy Allan, Jayden Hayward and Dean Budd. Dean was also retiring but after eight years with the club, and captaining Italy three times, he was one of those who wasn't going to be given a proper send-off either.

Benetton present jerseys to each departing player in a ceremony after the last home game of the season. That didn't happen, for obvious reasons, but instead we took a boat out to an island off Venice where the supporters cooked a meal for the whole squad, with a barbecue, pasta, salads and desserts, and presented the guys who were leaving with jerseys. That was a nice touch. Given there were going to be empty stadiums for over a year, we couldn't have asked for much more than that.

We also had 'a leaving party' with the whole squad. Antonio Rizzi, Tito Tebaldi, Nasi Manu and Marco Fuser were also moving on. A popular outdoor bar called "Dazio" with a garden area, which I thought looked like something from the film "The Great Gatsby" on a very small scale of course, was booked by some of us that were leaving. Everyone came and brought their families on a glorious day, with the temperatures staying warm into the evening.

For Cords and I, it was a hugely emotional night too as we had a good group of friends through the club. We were very lucky with our time in Treviso because we really did find good people, several of whom were also moving on. It was a salute to the progress of the previous years and also to the future.

All in all there were many goodbyes from our neighbours, local people we knew, teammates, ex-teammates and fans. We could not leave though without making one more trip back to where it all started up in Udine. There, surrounded by all the people I grew so fond of from when I first moved over, we had one last meal together before we said our goodbyes. We flew back to Ireland a few days later at the end of July 2020 just before I was about to start my ninth year in Italy.

•••••

Our Aer Lingus flight was cancelled for a day because there was an insufficient number of passengers. There were only 15 people on our flight and we were all seated in the middle of the plane. We all wore masks and before landing there was an announcement to follow the Covid-19 guidelines set out by the Irish Government. But, after picking up our luggage and going through passport control, you could do as you pleased. We found that quite surprising as Italy was much stricter.

We landed in Dublin for the first time since the Aviva game almost a year previously and were picked up by Cordelia's brother, George, who drove north to Ballyscullion. Cordelia's family have outhouses as part of their wedding business and we were able to isolate there for two weeks.

Even though four seasons with Benetton is not necessarily a

long time, ultimately, as well as playing for Italy, I played more for Benetton than I did for Leinster.

Overall, my time at Benetton was really positive so I wanted to leave with as best a relationship with the club as I could as both myself and Cordelia genuinely called it our home.

I did see Antonio Pavanello before I left and, to the club's credit, they gave me and the other departing players crystal glasses as thanks for our service.

I told him that I would like to see him in the future and stay in contact, because I really would like to revisit Treviso and the club one day. It was a very amicable conversation. I didn't want to be angry with the club. I am involved in visually impaired rugby and Benetton have opened up their pitches to help me with that. If I left on bad terms things like that would have been harder to initiate. I did give 'Pava' some feedback on what the club can do to improve!

But we left on good terms. There was no bitterness or bad blood on either side. That was important for me.

FOURTEEN

Looking Forward

Monday, August 15th, 2022

AS CAPTAIN of the British & Irish Lions tour of 1974 to South Africa, Willie John McBride devised the '99' call.

This was the cue for all the Lions players on the pitch to join in a mass brawl if a fight started, both to demonstrate their refusal to be intimidated by the Springboks, and make it virtually impossible for a referee to single out one player and send him off.

In the third and penultimate Test of the series in Port Elizabeth, the Scottish lock Gordon Brown punched his opposite number Johan de Bruyn, who was playing his one and only match for the Springboks that day, and caused his glass eye to pop out. The match had to be stopped as players and officials searched for the glass eye in front of 55,000 fans.

When it was found de Bruyn popped the glass eye back in, leaving tufts of grass sticking out from his eye for the remainder of the game. The Test was played in the Boet Erasmus Stadium and was famously dubbed the 'Battle of Boet Erasmus'.

In 2001, shortly before Gordon Brown died of cancer at the age of 53, de Bruyn surprised him by flying to a special reception in London, at which Fergus Slattery was Master of Ceremonies. During the reception, de Bruyn presented Brown with his glass eye from that match 27 years previously, which he had embedded into a decanter.

This story embodies rugby's capacity to build deep, life-long connections. There wasn't a dry eye in the room, as the saying goes, and Brown died six weeks later.

My story is unique.

I became the first rugby player to play at various levels with the goggles, be it what is now the United Rugby Championship, the Champions Cup, the European Challenge Cup and international level, and also in the campaigns to have them approved by World Rugby and all the main unions and federations. But I am not alone.

Barrie McDermott had a distinguished rugby league career with Leeds Rhinos, among others, Great Britain and Ireland, despite losing one eye. The Fijian 7s player, Masivesi Dakuwaqa, won an Olympic Gold medal in Rio de Janeiro in 2016 and now plays for Montpellier in the Top 14 despite being partially blind in one eye. He has on occasion worn the rugby goggles during games.

I've also written about Florian Cazenave, the French scrum-half, who the last I heard, played for Vannes in the ProD2, and even the All Blacks' backrower Ardie Savea made it known publicly that he had eye issues during the 2019 World Cup and did use the rugby goggles in a group game against Canada.

Gavin Quinnell, the son of Derek and younger brother of Scott and Craig (who were all Welsh internationals), was not so fortunate. He lost the sight in one eye due to a gouging incident during a match for Llanelli in October 2010 and was forced to retire as a result, when he was just 26.

In 2019 a freak training accident caused the 25-year-old Welsh Dragons prop Jack Cosgrove to lose his sight in one eye and he also had to retire immediately as a result.

On a separate note, during training sessions in the 2007 World Cup in Marseille, the All Blacks were photographed wearing eye patches, which they used to improve their hand-eye coordination. The GAA introduced what are called chin-up goggles to improve players' depth perception and peripheral vision by reducing lower eyesight.

Such initiatives and ideas concerning lack of sight or depth perception highlight the progress being made in these areas by various sports, and also, perhaps, a greater acceptance of players who manage to continue playing despite visual impairments. More progress needs to be made though. When the goggles first emerged, a newspaper ran a rather disparaging headline in March 2014 which read: 'Biggles meets rugby in new eye-flying goggles'.

Some fans apparently had a field day on social media as well when I played for Italy in the autumn of 2017. European rugby had been exposed to the goggles more regularly by then, but they still seemed to surprise other supporters who weren't aware of their development.

I try not to look at social media but whenever a sportsman or woman is a 'first' in something they can bear the brunt of jibes, and I definitely was on the receiving end of some mockery: 'What the hell is he doing with these goggles?' 'It's embarrassing.' 'How bad can Italy get if they have a guy who needs goggles to help them play rugby.'

When the goggles first came on to the scene and I began reaching higher and higher levels of course I was met with praise and admiration, but other people wanted to put me down, and laugh and mock what is essentially my disability.

But I was prepared to take the brunt of that and be the scapegoat if it then helped other people, because whenever I talk to kids whose parents ask me to give them words of wisdom, usually the most common request is for me to encourage them because they feel self-conscious about wearing them.

I think the prejudice against players who wear goggles is

founded in some popular idea of image, as opposed to anything regarding their actual functionality.

On the pitch there was some, if less, derision.

Indeed, in one Pro12 game against Connacht in the Sportsground one of their players, in clearing me out, hit me with his shoulder and it connected front on with the goggles. I remember it distinctly. It probably would have led to him receiving a red card today.

He immediately said: "Oh sorry."

I replied: "It's rugby".

I didn't want to have that sympathy from people, least of all opponents, because then you're not there on merit. Some people no doubt noted that, as Conor O'Shea is Irish, there may have been some favouritism in him picking me. But I knew deep down that my selections for Italy were on merit and performance. I didn't want favouritism or special treatment.

That incident in the Sportsground always stuck with me. I wanted to be smashed. I wanted to play against the Springboks, knowing they didn't care about my goggles. I didn't want a soft approach, or opponents holding back. I wouldn't have found out half as much about the goggles if I had just kept playing at a lower level.

I did receive some verbal slights from players. "I've got the pussy" springs to mind, but generally players were fine and rarely said anything. In truth, I'd say they were just baffled by them.

You always heard stuff from the crowd but that just egged you on, although that was another reason why I loved playing in Italy. They only saw me after I started back playing, so it was never "Ian with the goggles", whereas when we went away sometimes it was different, with "Goggles, you're shit" being one shout that sticks in the memory. There was no pattern, or rhyme or reason to the verbal abuse. Some were in England, some in Ireland, or wherever. But people shout what they want and I'm sure a heck of a lot worse comments have been aimed at players.

I'd hope my family didn't hear many comments. I wouldn't have been out there on those pitches from 2014 onwards but for them. When you have a major setback, it quickly makes you realise what people you have around you and will help you in your time of need.

I'm just really fortunate that my family were able to do that, and I know I haven't won many medals or trophies in comparison with many of my former teammates, but I also know that I won the biggest battle.

That is why I will never be resentful towards rugby. Many people in my position might have turned against rugby or even hated the game. But my passion and love for the game remains, and that would not have been possible without my family. They kept me believing, and as a result we turned a negative into a positive. No stone was left unturned with regard to training methods, understanding the goggles and all the campaigns against the various unions and federations just to have them permitted.

Cordelia gave birth to our first child, Malachy, on December 16th 2020 and plenty of people ask me, because of what happened to me and the concussion issues in the sport, whether I would be happy for my son to play rugby. Certainly, I would encourage him to play sport and, based on my experiences as a boy, I think it is important to dip your toes into different sports. It's a good way of learning how different teams can work. If you were to play tennis, Gaelic or hockey, they certainly require different abilities and skills, so I'd hope that he would enjoy sport and be a happy and healthy 'outdoorsy' boy.

Whatever route he does go down I will support him but I admit I would like him to play a team sport more than an individual sport. In individual sports you do have your team around you, but it can be a lonely place and whatever you achieve is based very much on your own performance.

That is true for a team sport as well, but teammates can really pick you up and you'll never find another job in the world where you're generally surrounded by 40 or 50 players who want to do the same thing and are all in it together. I think that's very hard to replicate in life. You also make lifelong friends so if Malachy shows an interest that's why I would encourage him, based on my experiences, to play a team sport. Then again, he could end up being an artist like his grandmother on Cordelia's side. So, who knows?

However, I certainly wouldn't put him off based on my experiences. I am, perhaps, lucky in that I have only suffered mild concussions. Since restarting my career in Italy I have failed only one concussion test.

In lifestyle, Treviso was a perfect fit for us, as Benetton was for me as a club. I trained and played with a good group of people. There was a good atmosphere in La Ghirada and it was really exciting being part of a club that was changing its culture and progressing.

Even though we weren't winning trophies, there were loads of little milestones that had never been reached before; learning how to win away, beating Leinster at the RDS, going on winning streaks and reaching the play-offs for the first time.

Off the pitch we built a new life in Italy, learned the language, made new friends for life that we would never otherwise have had. There is an Italian side to me that I never want to lose and my Irish friends slag me because I still do Italian gestures.

I speak to Malachy in Italian and want him to learn the language. I would love to move back in the future. When that will be I do not know. But we absolutely fell in love with Italy and its way of life. We have friends there whom I consider almost family, particularly the people in Udine. When I moved over there first they helped me hugely and I will always keep in touch with them.

I became eligible to play for Italy due to the three-year residency ruling, which has since been increased to five years, and made my debut for Italy on the same day Bundee Aki made his debut for Ireland.

I'm always of the opinion that the players should never be blamed for the ruling because they're only adhering to the laws of the game. Yes, there will be some people who are wholeheartedly against it, but I am all for it for obvious reasons.

I believe it is instructive to consider what players like Aki, James Lowe, Jamison Gibson-Park and CJ Stander have given to rugby in Ireland. Their contribution runs a bit deeper than just playing for the Irish international team.

They have bought into the culture which the indigenous players have established and contributed to a winning mentality with their skills and attitude and I don't think anyone can question their commitment both to their provinces and the Irish rugby team. The proof is in their performances, but also in the way they have embedded themselves in their communities.

The outpouring of emotion and gratitude toward CJ Stander within Ireland when he retired after nine seasons with Munster was also proof of that. Bundee Aki is about to enter his eighth season with Connacht, where he is adored by young kids, in the same way Stander was in Munster, as are Lowe – with his long hair and engaging character, and Gibson-Park with Leinster. They have inspired young kids to play the game and all of them, in their own unique way, have had a positive impact on Irish rugby, from grass roots to provincial and international level.

That those guys helped Ireland to beat New Zealand is

testament to how good they are and how much positivity and quality they can bring to a team.

I can understand both sides of the residency rule argument now, whereas I might not if I hadn't played for Italy. But, insofar as I can see, the Irish players I have named have become symbols for young, aspiring rugby players and from a professional standpoint, they're also bloody good rugby players who are performing to the best of their ability for their provinces and Ireland. And that's all that you can ask from them.

When you look back at what they've contributed, on a professional standpoint, to Irish rugby, is that a positive or a negative? It's 100 per cent positive.

•••••

I would hope that after almost ten years in Italy they would appreciate my total commitment to the cause of Italian rugby as well.

Italian rugby has had plenty of negative press due to their results. Even their continuing participation in the Six Nations has been questioned. Yet here was a Federation that stood up for the goggles. In that regard, they were a truly pioneering rugby nation, and it portrays Italian rugby in a very positive light. They were able to help a player like me, or others that were in a similar position, to pursue their careers where other unions would not have done so.

The best way I could repay that support and faith was to

produce my best performance for my club and my adopted country. For me, honestly, putting on the blue jersey was the biggest honour of my rugby career. As someone born in Dublin and Ireland, who came through St Columba's and the Leinster academy, I have no qualms about saying that.

Yes, our winning percentages were not fantastic but for me it went a lot deeper than results. Adopting me represented the fighting attitude in Italian rugby. They did everything in their power to facilitate me as a player and that also trickles down to the clubs that I played for, whether it was Leonorso, Viadana, Zebre or Benetton. During the prolonged campaign to have the goggles approved, the Federation even provided me with special insurance for one of the games. They didn't need to do that, but they wanted to help me and that's why I am so attached to them.

Italian rugby has also been criticised for having an over-reliance on players who qualified through the residency rule, but I don't agree that this is the case anymore.

Like Joey Carbery and Jeremy Loughman moving to Ireland when they were kids, Cherif Traoré moved to Italy when he was seven and Ion Neculai did so at the age of two. Only four Italian players who qualified on the residency ruling as adults played in the Six Nations, one more than Ireland, and one less than Scotland.

Only three played in the win over Wales, and in the summer games against Portugal, Romania and Georgia, only two of the 33-man squad, Hame Faiva and Toa Halafihi, fell into this category.

Definitely, there has been a long search for an out-half, which is why Paolo Garbisi is really important for Italy because he's come through the system. In fact, the vast majority of the current squad were born in Italy and have come through the Italian ranks. There has been a greater emphasis on developing Italian players, just as France did a few years ago for the 2023 World Cup.

World Rugby changed the residency ruling from three to five years at the end of 2021, and this is a tricky one. Three and five years are both relatively long periods in professional playing careers and I think only time will prove what difference this change will make and how much the numbers will be affected in, say, ten years' time. Like many law changes, it may even create unforeseen problems as the bigger or wealthier countries pinch players from the poorer countries at a younger age.

Three years is still a good chunk of a professional player's career, especially if you move abroad at 26 or 27. Unless you are an exceptional talent and lucky with your body, you could be looking at four or five years of international rugby. That's still not many years really. Furthermore, if the change to a five-year qualification through residency had been made sooner, I may never have played for Italy as I would not have been eligible until 2019 instead of 2017.

Not all residency rule players receive a positive reaction but I was always well received in Italy. I couldn't have asked for a better reception from players, coaches, supporters, journalists and pundits. There was no negativity and what made me really happy in Italy was that I was just seen as Ian McKinley the rugby player whereas in Ireland I think there was still the view, based on sympathy, that Ian McKinley never reached his potential.

I started with a completely new slate in Italy. I had no sort of baggage with me. Everything was very positive. If I didn't have a fantastic game, I'm sure fans would have written things or said things. A couple of fans here or there would have said things to me on the street, but that's pretty normal.

There was never any hostility because I was not Italian born and I was competing for the out-half position with Tommy Allen and Carlo Canna. We each pushed each other which is what every player wants.

Certainly, I one hundred per cent support the residency rule. My family roots will always be in Ireland but when I'm doing my TV work I am always supporting Italy if they are playing Ireland. If Ireland are playing anyone else, of course I will support Ireland, but I am invested in Italian rugby and hope to do whatever I can in the future to help the game in Italy advance.

They opened their doors to me and gave me an opportunity that others would not have done. They were there for me when I needed them, and I would have hoped I gave my best, both in a coaching and a playing capacity. We left on good terms, which means I would love to help them in the future. I embedded myself in Italian culture and would want my son, one day, to experience an Italian lifestyle. It's a wonderful place to live.

I'm living in Northern Ireland at the moment but I always say I am very fortunate to have two homes, and I don't say that lightly. I truly do mean that. If the injury had never happened, would I ever have moved to Italy? It's very unlikely.

My time at Treviso did not end the way I would have wanted. But how many players do get to have the perfect send off? I was certainly at peace with my decision to retire, even though I was still only 31 and had some good rugby left in me.

When I spoke with Philip about the idea of stopping, he said: "Do you have any regrets?"

Ultimately many sports people will have regrets. That's just the nature of the beast. You can't win all the battles, even though you want to win all of them. But I know that I will never hold a grudge against the game. For example, I enjoyed going to an Ulster training session a couple of days ago but in the years immediately after my accident, if the sessions involved players of my own age or older, I didn't like being there. I would have been so angry watching some of my old teammates and friends training and playing. I still enjoyed the sport, but I resented that everyone else was doing it and not me.

I'd still love to be doing a few things out there, but now I am totally at peace both with watching that training session and retiring.

I think that's the greatest gift considering what happened. My life could have gone a completely different way. In that sense, I suppose, learning how to play with the goggles and returning to the professional game was my healing process. I am totally healed, and more. The deep frustration in the years immediately after my accident was thinking I would never experience the highs and lows of playing in the Champions Cup and international rugby. But I've since gone and done all of that and more.

So, there's no bad blood, animosity or negativity.

If there's a challenge in front of me, I am so much more confident in my ability to approach it and overcome it, and it would be impossible for me to repay my family completely for that.

I did want to repay the faith shown in me by my family, and by the Italian Federation, through producing my best performances on the field and trying to enjoy it as best I could.

There are certain games I wish I had played better or that we had won, but not one single sports person has ever had the perfect career, or doesn't have moments, mistakes or defeats that didn't hurt.

Roger Federer has won 20 Grand Slam titles but I am sure if you ask him if he had any regrets he'd probably say, or think, 'Well, I wish I'd got 21'. Sports people are like kids in a sweet shop. They always want that little bit more, and I do too.

But I'm also realistic that from where my career was to where it reached, in the space of time that happened, was pretty good. From being on that operating table and knowing, the next day, that the vision in my left eye was gone, to six years later and standing in Catania with an international jersey on me, brings a little perspective. That was pretty good. I know my family and I did absolutely everything that we could to try and reach that level. I can rest easy with that. I am okay with it, whereas for some people retirement might be very difficult. Maybe my perspective is partially shaped by the experience I went through. Maybe that's why I could retire without a heavy heart the second time round. I am not draped with medals on my chest, but inside my own skin I do feel like a winner.

The decision to come back to Ireland was also looking forward to the next stage in my life, which revolves around family and going into coaching.

I definitely want to coach as a full-time career in the future. At the moment I am the head coach of the Rainey Old Boys senior team and I am a sales rep for medical instruments and sell eye instruments for cataract and retina surgeries.

I am also working on visually impaired projects, more on the charitable side of things, which I absolutely love.

As somebody once said to me recently at a training session: "Ian, you were bloody lucky that you got to be in the one per cent of the rugby world which is professional rugby, because when you're here looking at all of us, we're in the 99 per cent who don't play professional rugby."

It's true, and after being in that little bubble, you're exposed to what the vast bulk of rugby really is, which is community spirit and people pulling together for a good cause. That was evident in the recent IMART (mixed ability) World Cup in Cork in June this year; seeing families and players coming together for the greater good within rugby.

All those initiatives interest me, not just because of what happened to me but also because of my family background and upbringing. I like helping people and making people aware that with visual impairment you can still be active in sport. You don't need to shy away from it. While I have more involvement with that side of the game, I am still involved with mixed ability rugby as well.

Starting out I wanted to be a rugby player and now I want to be a rugby coach. In what capacity I still don't know yet but what I learned during Covid-19 was that you can't be a one-trick pony. Having different strings to your bow is important; just learning about different things, as in eye operations for example. I have undergone four of them but knowing the ins and outs of what they involve is, for me, interesting. I guess I'm in a learning process now that I've retired again.

People often ask me: 'Do you wish the injury didn't happen to you?"

I cannot definitively say "yes" or "no".

Of course, the accident meant I could never fulfil the dream of putting on the green jersey at senior level, but there are things that I have gone on to achieve which I am very grateful for and otherwise would never have happened.

Working with various visually impaired rugby teams is one example. I work alongside Alex Bassan, of the Change

Foundation, which is based in England and is an award-winning charity created to improve the lives of marginalised young people.

They have the England VI (visually impaired) Roses team who are working with their Irish equivalent, and we started training sessions last year.

We have held a training session in Italy, although this is still in the very early stages, and have been in contact with the visually impaired rugby team associated with Cardiff Rugby.

I would never have met these people or teams if I hadn't had the accident and if you want to elevate your coaching levels I fully believe you have to teach a visually impaired rugby team because the lines of communication need to be spot on.

If, for example, you say: "Go and stand behind the cone there" some of the participants will respond: "Where's the cone?" You have to be very specific in how you relay information.

I've worked as an ambassador for Laureus Italy, the Italian branch of the global Laureus Sport For Good Foundation. They have hosted annual sports awards since 2000 which are akin to the Oscars of sports. I sold some of my rugby memorabilia after I retired, the proceeds of which went into the very first Laureus Foundation rugby project.

I probably would never have worked on television with Virgin Media but for my ability to give an Italian insight and perspective on their games, and I hope people enjoy, and are informed by, my punditry. I have also had the honour of being included in the sporting abroad section of the EPIC Irish Emigration Museum in Dublin along with other sporting greats. In Italy, I worked with the famous glasses company Carrera and their "driveyourstory" campaign and then there is my documentary "Look Beyond" produced by Aurora Vision. It is certainly surreal to have your face on the big screen but not only has it made it to the platforms of Netflix and Amazon Prime but amazingly it has been shown at the famous Cannes Film Festival.

Also, there are now roughly 2,500 players registered to use the goggles, which is an extraordinary number that gives me a huge amount of pride. You need a purpose to play and, of course, most of them want to compete and want to win. If there were rainy days when I couldn't see properly and we had a bad defeat, or alternatively the conditions were perfect and we had a good win, I tried not to become too low or too high based on results.

As my career was progressing, I realised I was also playing to inspire other visually impaired people and particularly young kids who perceive themselves differently if they wear goggles, when in fact it's totally normal and they can break through barriers. Yes, it can be more difficult but if you really want to do it, just keep working at it.

'Playing to Inspire' became my mantra for putting in so much hard work and training every day. That's what I tried to do, and I hope I inspired and encouraged a few people along the way.

Although I gave away plenty of my rugby memorabilia,

including jerseys, I have kept plenty too. The most important jersey is the one from my Test debut for Italy, and my other most cherished item is the goggles from that first Test – the first pair ever used at international level.

The jersey represents so much fight to get there. It really does.

That day when we played Fiji in Catania is the only time I wore that particular pair of goggles. I put them away and said: "They're my special pair." I don't have a wall to put them on, but I will one day.

I genuinely hope in the future that another player who requires the use of goggles will better the number of games that I played, will get more international caps and win a tournament wearing them.

I may have been the first, but I hope I'm not the last.

Acknowledgements

FIRST AND foremost, I would not be telling this story without the unbelievable assistance, love and support of my immediate family. As the book points out, I am blessed to have a very close family and I would like to mention Mum, Dad, Andrew, Emma and Philip for all they have done for me.

Philip in particular went above and beyond the realms of what one sibling should have to do for another. He was incredible. He was the one with the ideas and the drive to make it happen and to break down the barriers that needed to come down. He was the catalyst and the spearhead and I am immensely proud of him and grateful that he is my brother.

I am also eternally grateful to the country of Italy and its rugby community for the way it opened their arms and took me and Cordelia in as one of their own.

The support, friendship and encouragement we received helped make a difficult time far easier than it could have been. I just loved Italy so much – the food, the language, the culture, everything – and it has left a long and lasting impression on us both.

To the teams, the coaches, the lads I played with and against; thank you for the challenge, the guidance, the competition, the memories, the laughter, the friendships and the camaraderie. There is nowhere quite like a rugby dressing room after a tight win, surrounded by your good mates, all of whom have put themselves on the line for each other. It is a feeling that you never forget and will forever bring a smile to my face.

I would also like to thank Gerry Thornley. There are a lot of very impressive rugby journalists in Ireland, and Gerry sits at the very top of that list. I have known Gerry for many, many years, his dedication, patience and counsel have all been invaluable and I would not have wanted anybody else to help put my life story into words.

At my publishers Reach Sport, I'd like to thank Paul Dove and editor Chris Brereton for their hard work in moulding and shaping the story into the book you're holding today.

Finally, I need to express my love and gratitude for my incredible wife Cordelia and son Malachy. Cordelia has been right next to me along the way and her love and understanding has helped me through many long nights and many difficult moments while Malachy has enriched our lives in so many ways since he came along.